CHEAP
EATS
in ITALY

SANDRA A. GUSTAFSON

CHRONICLE BOOKS

SAN FRANCISCO

Printed in the United States of America

Library of Congress Cataloging-in-Publication Data
Gustafson, Sandra.
    Cheap eats in Italy / Sandra A. Gustafson.
        p. cm.
    Includes index.
    ISBN 0-8118-0207-8 (pbk.)
        1. Restaurants, lunch rooms, etc.—Italy—Florence—Guidebooks.
2. Restaurants, lunch rooms, etc.—Italy—Rome—Guidebooks.
3. Restaurants, lunch rooms, etc.—Italy—Venice—Guidebooks.
I. Title.
TX907.5.I8G87 1993
647.9545—dc20   92-28092
                                                        CIP

Editing: Carolyn Miller
Cover design: Robin Weiss
Cover photograph: Debra Lande
Cover map: Historic Urban Plans, Ithaca, NY
Book design: Words & Deeds

Distributed in Canada by
Raincoast Books
112 East Third Avenue
Vancouver, B.C. V5T 1C8

10 9 8 7 6 5 4 3 2 1

Chronicle Books
275 Fifth Street
San Francisco, California 94103

FOR PETE

CONTENTS

To the Reader   6

How to Use *Cheap Eats in Italy*   8

Tips on How to Have Cheap Eats in Italy   9

General Information about Italian Dining   11
    When to Eat   11
        Breakfast   11
        Lunch   11
        Dinner   11
    Where to Eat   12
    The Italian Menu   13
        How to Read an Italian Menu   14
    Chiuso (Closed)   15
    Holidays   15
    Reservations   15
    Smoking   16
    Paying the Bill   16
        Prices   16
        Cover Charge (*Pane e coperto*)   16
        Service Charge   17

Restaurants   19
    Florence   20
    Rome   57
    Venice   101

Quick Reference Guide   141
    Big Splurge   142
    Glossary of Words, Phrases, and Menu Terms   144

Readers' Comments   153

Index   154

TO THE READER

In Florence you think, in Rome you pray, and in Venice you love.
Italian proverb

From the Middle Ages onward, Italians have been trend setters at the table. They were the first people to use the fork, the first to wash their hands before a meal, and one of the first to make a point of using the freshest of ingredients in their food preparations. Few countries in the Western world have given so much to so many. Just think of all the foods you love, and you will probably find that a majority of them are Italian: pasta, pizza, balsamic vinegar, Parmesan cheese, sun-dried tomatoes, porcini mushrooms, polenta, osso buco, prosciutto, minestrone—the list is endless. When we want satisfaction, comfort, or pure enjoyment, we eat Italian because it tastes like Mama's food, no matter what nationality Mama is.

To an Italian, life is meant to be lived fully, and food is not merely sustenance, but a work of art to be enjoyed and relished on a meal-to-meal basis. A full meal is carefully divided into courses of *antipasti* (appetizers), *primo piatto* (first course), *secondo piatto* (second course), and *dolce* (dessert). Wine is always on the table, and so is mineral water. If you overindulge, a shot of the strong herbal mix Fernet-Branca, available in most bars, will set you straight in no time.

In the last thirty years, Italy has gone through a complete economic transformation and is now the world's fifth-largest industrial power. As a result, prices have tripled, the dollar is down, and inflation is on a runaway track. *Nothing* is cheap in Italy—and certainly not the food. That romantic trattoria where only a few years ago an al fresco dinner with a bottle of good wine would cost $15 no longer exists. If you want a cheap Italian meal, you had better stay home and go to your local pizza parlor. It won't be as good as the wood-fired pizza at Gioia Mia in Rome, but I can assure you it will be *much* cheaper.

What to do? Don't worry—just use *Cheap Eats in Italy*. But *please* be aware that this book is not a listing of the cheapest places to eat in Florence, Rome, and Venice. It is, rather, your guide in each city to good-quality food with a realistic cost-to-value ratio. It will lead you to pleasant meals in all categories, from Big Splurges to picnics on the piazza, by showing you how to plan and select your dining for the maximum value for the minimum outlay.

In doing the research for this book, I spent months in Italy, walking over 450 miles in every type of weather, checking on more than six hundred addresses, and eating meals that ranged from poor and indifferent to delightful and gourmet.

The result is this edition of *Cheap Eats in Italy*, which suggests more than 150 dining possibilities for people who enjoy good food and eating well while spending less. In each write-up I have described the atmosphere and decor of the restaurant; the other diners; how the food is prepared, presented, and tastes; and what it all costs. The recommended dishes are included to give an idea of what the restaurant does best. Because most menus in these three cities reflect four seasons of the year, it is possible that many of the dishes I describe may not be on the menu when you visit. The subject of the many fine Italian wines is one I do not cover, though I do comment on the house wines and tell you if they are drinkable or not.

Whether you are going for business or sightseeing, I urge you to travel with an open mind. When you leave home, don't expect to encounter your way of life or favorite soul foods until you return. Enjoy where you are, the people, the sights, the sounds, and even the smells. Sample a wide variety of the food, smile, and try your best to roll with the punches that are bound to come your way. If you can see the humor in a difficult situation, you will come home a more knowledgeable person, with a lifetime of happy memories.

By using *Cheap Eats in Italy*, I hope you will return with some of the best memories of all: those of good meals in wonderful settings. If I have been able to help you do this, I will consider my job well done. I want to hear from all of you—until then, *buona fortuna* and, above all, *buon appetito*.

How to Use
Cheap Eats in Italy

Each listing in *Cheap Eats in Italy* includes the following information: the name and address of the establishment, the area of the city in which it is located, the telephone number, the days it is open and closed and the hours of service, whether reservations are necessary, which credit cards are accepted, the average price of a three-course à la carte meal, the price of the *menù turistico* (set-price meal), what the cover and service charges are, and whether or not English is spoken.

The following abbreviations are used in the listings:

To indicate annual vacation closing:
    No annual closing   NAC

To indicate credit cards accepted:
    American Express   AMEX
    Diners Club   DC
    MasterCard or Access   MC
    Visa   V

At the end of the restaurant listings, you will find a Quick Reference Guide. This lists Big Splurge restaurants for those with more flexible budgets, and a glossary of menu and restaurant terms as well as a page for your comments.

TIPS ON HOW TO HAVE CHEAP EATS IN ITALY

1. If you see a headwaiter standing at the door, tour buses parked outside, or an empty restaurant during prime time, keep going.

2. Always read the menu posted outside before going in. This prevents you from being seated before finding that you do not like anything on the menu, or worse, that the prices are too high.

3. Remember where you are when you are ordering, and stay within the limits of the chef's ability. Don't expect gourmet fare in a snack bar, and don't go to a nice restaurant and order only a salad and a glass of wine.

4. Carefully consider the daily special or the house specialties. You can bet they will be the best the chef can do that day, and 100 percent fresh.

5. Most main courses on à la carte menus are not garnished. Vegetables and salads will be extra.

6. Beware of dishes on the à la carte menu (such as fish or Florentine beef steaks) or anything marked *S.Q.* or *L 4,000 hg. S.Q.* means that you will be charged according to the total weight of the food ordered. *L 4,000 hg* means you will pay 4,000 lire *per* hectogram (3 ½ ounces).

7. To keep the tab lower on an à la carte meal, skip the *antipasti* and desserts and head for the pastas and main courses.

8. The cheapest lunches are those eaten while standing in a snack bar or sitting in a piazza munching on fixings bought fresh from the local market or deli. In snack bars and cafeterias, arrive early for best selection.

9. Remember that the cover charge is *per person* and that the service charge is a percentage of the total bill. Also, remember that *the service charge is the tip.* When you add the two on top of a full meal with wine, dessert, and coffee, the bottom line could cause heartburn.

10. Almost every *menù turistico* (set-price meal) includes the cover and service charges.

11. Watch out for hidden costs on any *prezzo fisso* menu. This is a type of set-price menu, but usually the cover, service, and beverages are extra.

12. If you sit in a *caffè*, you will be charged more than if you stand at the bar. In addition, if you sit outside, your bill could be even higher.

13. By law, restaurants must indicate when frozen food is used. Most often you will find that if anything is frozen, it will be the fish. If there is an asterisk (*) by a menu item, it is frozen. Just to be on the safe side, ask if the fish is *fresco* (fresh) or *congelato* (frozen).

14. *Always, always* look over your bill and add it up yourself. Mistakes are rampant.

General Information
about Italian Dining

Everything you see I owe to spaghetti.

—Sophia Loren

WHEN TO EAT

BREAKFAST (*LA COLAZIONE* OR *LA PRIMA COLAZIONE*)

Hotels and *pensione* usually serve a Continental breakfast that consists of a choice of coffee, tea, hot chocolate, fresh rolls, butter, and preserves. Cheap Eaters will ask their hotel to deduct this cost—sometimes as much as $15 per person—from their bill (yes, you read that correctly!) and will eat their breakfast at a bar or *caffè* between 7 and 10 A.M. In addition to the price being at least half of what a hotel will charge, the coffee will be better, the pastry fresher, and the local scene far more interesting. If you sit at a table, prices may be from 50 percent to 250 percent *more* than if you stand at the bar with all the Italians.

LUNCH (*PRANZO* OR *COLAZIONE*)

Lunch starts at 12:30 or 1:00 and lasts anywhere from thirty minutes to three hours, depending on where you eat. The meal can be anything from a quick sandwich eaten standing at a corner snack bar, to a full-blown four- or five-course meal ending with a long coffee in the sunshine—one of the true pleasures of eating in Italy. Time, cost, calories, location, and hunger are the factors that help you decide what to do for lunch. Sandwiches are available in a *paninoteca*, a bar selling sandwiches either made to order or ready made and found displayed under napkins in a self-service case. If you are staying in one place for a few days, it is fun to become a "local" by eating your lunch each day in the same small restaurant or trattoria. The first day you will be treated with politeness. The second, your waiter will be pleased to see you, and on the third, you will be treated like a "regular" by everyone there, and your waiter will already know what type of wine you like. Try it—you will be surprised.

DINNER (*CENA*)

Dinner is served from 7:30 on. If you want to eat with other foreigners, reserve a table for 7:30. If you want a more Italian experience, dine at

9:00 or later. Most places do not require a coat and tie, but Italians do dress with casual elegance when they eat out, so please leave your jogging shoes and T-shirts in the hotel room.

WHERE TO EAT

At one time there was a distinct difference between a trattoria and a *ristorante*, based on the type of clientele and the prices charged. Now they are virtually interchangeable. A trattoria is generally a family-run affair with Mamma or Papà in the kitchen, carrying on the old ways. The decor and menu are simple and the prices are *slightly* less than in a ristorante.

Fast-food *italiano* has taken hold. The *Tavola calda*—meaning "hot table"—is a stand-up snack bar open all day. *Rosticcerie* offer hot and cold dishes to eat there or take out. The dishes are priced individually or sold by weight. Self-service snack counters in coffee bars sell sandwiches and sometimes a hot special dish. You will also encounter the *pizzeria*, which specializes, naturally, in pizza. The *latteria* sells cheese, yogurt, and other milk products; a *gelateria* serves ice cream, and a *pasticceria* is where you go for a pastry. At *il forno* you can buy bread, and at an *alimentari, salumeria,* or *gastronomia* you can buy cold cuts, cheese, wine, bread, mineral water, and other food to put together a picnic in the piazza or back at your hotel. For a glass or two of fine wine and a light meal, the *enoteca*, or wine bar, is the place to remember.

Caffè are often called bars to remind you that you are supposed either to stand up, or to pay more for anything consumed sitting at a table. An Italian bar is much more than a place to drink coffee or alcoholic beverages. Here you can eat breakfast, have a snack, make phone calls, read the local paper, listen to soccer matches, meet your neighbor or lover, or argue over politics. Everyone watches everybody else, and this is called minding your business. If there is a black and white "T" (for *tabacco*) displayed outside, you can buy cigarettes, matches, salt, some toiletries, stamps, and bus tickets. No wonder these places are on almost every corner and so popular.

What kind of coffee should you order in a *caffè*? The possibilities are bewildering to most Americans, but here is a list of the most popular caffeine-laden drinks.

caffè	A small cup of very strong coffee like espresso
caffè Americano	American-style coffee, but stronger
caffè corretto	Coffee "corrected" with a shot of grappa, cognac, or other spirit

caffè freddo	Iced coffee
caffè Hag	Decaffeinated coffee
caffè latte	Hot milk mixed with coffee and served in a glass for breakfast
caffè macchiato	Espresso "stained" with a drop of milk
cappuccino	Strong coffee infused with steamed milk and drunk until lunch, but never, never after a meal
granitadi caffè con panne	Iced coffee with whipped cream
latte caldo	Hot milk

Like the French, the Italians *never* ever drink coffee or tea with a meal. An espresso is often ordered after a meal, but tea is considered a between-meal drink, or one to be used for medicinal purposes.

THE ITALIAN MENU

The most important thing to keep in mind about eating in any Italian restaurant is not to let the length of the menu frighten you. Think where you are and order accordingly. If you are in a casual trattoria, you probably won't be expected to order every course. The better the restaurant, however, the more you will be expected to order. Going to a nice restaurant for lunch and ordering a salad or a plate of pasta and a glass of wine is considered bad form. When you consider the cover and service charges on top, it will not be a Cheap Eat either. If you want a light meal, or a real Cheap Eat, go to a cafeteria, snack bar, or wine bar, or dine al fresco with a picnic you have put together yourself.

Some restaurants offer a *menù turistico* at an all-inclusive price. Don't let the name turn you off—it really is just a fixed-price menu that at the very least includes pasta, an entrée, and vegetable or salad; at the most, it will include all of these, plus dessert and wine. *Pane e coperto* (cover) and *servizio* (service) almost always are included. If you order this meal, you will avoid all the charges that will otherwise be tacked onto the final bill. While this is the Cheap Eat way to go, the quality and quantity might not be up to the standard of an à la carte meal. You will not have the finest beef or soft-shell crabs, nor will you taste the chef's finest efforts. You will get a filling, if slightly boring meal. Warning: A restaurant may post a *menù turistico* but not give it to you unless you ask for it.

In addition to the *menù turistico*, you will see *prezzo fisso* menus. These are also fixed-price menus, but with some hidden charges. Generally they do not include the cover or service charges, and seldom the dessert or beverage.

Whatever you order anywhere in Italy, be sure to add up the bill yourself and be certain you are not being charged for cover and/or service when they are included, or paying for courses and dishes you did not order.

HOW TO READ AN ITALIAN MENU

Antipasti	Appetizers
Minestre or *primi piatti*	Soups (*ministra* means soup and so does *zuppa*), *gnocchi*, *risotto*, pasta
Uova	Eggs, *frittate*, omelettes
Pesce	Fish
Piatti del giorno or *secondi piatti*	Dishes of the day, main courses, entrées
Contorni, legumi, verdure; insalate	Vegetable side dishes, salads
Formaggi	Cheeses
Frutta	Fruit
Dolci	Desserts: cakes, pies, custards
Gelati	Ice creams
Pane e coperto	Bread and cover charge *per person*
Servizio	Service charge (10 to 15 percent of the total bill)

CHIUSO (CLOSED)

All eating and drinking establishments have a regular *giorno di chiusura*: the one or two days a week they are closed. Due to holidays, local customs, the ever-present threat of strikes *(scioperi)*, yearly vacations, restoration, and much more that the non-Italian could never fathom, the one place you really wanted to try may be closed. *Cheap Eats in Italy* listings tell you when the restaurant is open and closed. However, if you don't have a backup nearby, or it is important to you that you eat at this particular place, be sure to call ahead to double-check if they will be open.

Bakery, fruit and vegetable, and other food shops are all closed all day

Sunday and, in every city, one afternoon per week. Markets are open Monday through Saturday from 8:30 A.M. until 1:30 P.M.

HOLIDAYS

Very few restaurants in Italy are open 365 days a year. Most are closed one day a week and for vacations. Many close on some or all of the holidays below. Their policies always change, so to avoid disappointment, call ahead to check if your visit falls during these holiday times or in the months of December, January, or August.

New Year's Day	January 1
Epiphany	Varies; early in January
Good Friday	Varies
Easter	Varies
Easter Monday	Varies
Liberation Day	April 25
Labor Day	May 1
Assumption Day	August 15
All Saints' Day	November 1
Day of Immaculate Conception	December 8
Christmas Day	December 25
Santo Stefano	December 26

To Honor Patron Saints
Florence:
    St. John the Baptist   June 24
Rome:
    St. Peter's Day   June 29
Venice:
    St. Mark's Day   April 25

RESERVATIONS

Every *Cheap Eats in Italy* listing states the establishment's reservation policy. If reservations are suggested, please make them, because it is always better to arrive with reservations than to wish you had. Some places that are *very* busy will take them, but fail to honor the time. However, you should arrive on time, and if you can't make your reservation, please call to cancel.

SMOKING

Unfortunately, there is no Italian campaign saluting the health benefits of a smoke-free environment. During peak dining hours, especially in bars, caffès, and smaller restaurants and trattorias, the haze can get very thick. In the few places where smoking is prohibited or there is a special nonsmoking section, it will be noted in the *Cheap Eats in Italy* listing. Otherwise—*buona fortuna!*

PAYING THE BILL

Italian restaurant bills can be confusing. With the following advance knowledge, you will be better able to avoid the pitfalls of being overcharged or confused when *il conto* (the bill) is presented.

In two out of three restaurants, *caffès,* bars, snack bars, or wine bars, cash is king and plastic money (credit cards) is out. The notions of logic and convenience are new to most Italians, so remember cold hard cash (Italian lire, please), and don't leave home without it.

Before paying your bill, *always* add it up yourself and check your change. Mistakes in addition are very common.

PRICES

All *Cheap Eats in Italy* listings give the prices for à la carte dining and the *menù turistico* (fixed-price meal) if one is available. Almost every *menù turistico* includes three courses and the cover and service charges. À la carte prices rarely include the cover, but often the service is included. The à la carte prices in this book represent the *average* cost of a three-course meal—period. The prices quoted *do not include* the cover or service charge if there is one, or any beverages. In determining the average price, the cheapest and most expensive foods were avoided. Thus, you could spend more, or less, depending on what you decide to eat and drink. You should expect a margin of difference in the prices due to inflation, higher food and labor costs, the whims of owners, and the passage of time since this book was written.

COVER CHARGE (*PANE E COPERTO*)

Pane e coperto ("bread and cover") is not to be confused with the service charge. Almost every restaurant and trattoria in Italy charges the à la carte customer for bread, even if it is never touched, and for cover, which includes the table settings, flowers, and who knows what else. All menus *must* clearly state the cover charge, which is levied *per person* and listed separately on the bill, but is added to the total on which you will pay service. If you order the *menù turistico*, or eat standing at a snack bar counter, you will avoid the cover charge.

SERVICE CHARGE

Servizio incluso or *servizio compreso* means that the service charge is included in the price of the food. Otherwise, it has not been added and you will be expected to pay an added amount of from 10 to 15 percent of the total bill, cover included. To make it more difficult for the visitor, not every restaurant states in writing what its policy is. *Cheap Eats in Italy* has come to the rescue, because all listings state whether or not the service charge is included and, if it is not, how much you should add. "Service included" and "no service charge" mean you do not need to add extra unless you want to. It is important to remember that the service charge *is* the tip. If the service has been especially good and you are feeling generous, you can add an additional 5 percent for the waiter, but this is not mandatory. "No service charge" means it is *not* added and that it is up to you (the diner) to add it or not.

RESTAURANTS

FLORENCE

ROME

VENICE

FLORENCE

> Whichever way you turn, you are struck with picturesque beauty
> and faded splendors.
> —William Hazlitt,
> *Notes of a Journey Through France and Italy,* 1826

For nearly three centuries, from Giotto's time to Michelangelo's, Florence was the hub of the universe, producing countless art treasures and generating ideas that formed the cornerstone of twentieth century thought. Five centuries after the Renaissance was born here, Florence has become a victim of her own beauty and is in danger of being consumed by traffic, pollution, and crowds from the four corners of the planet. Streets designed to accommodate horse-drawn carriages and pedestrians now cope with cars, trucks, and hundreds of smog-inducing tour buses. Despite this, travelers continue to flock to Florence to immerse themselves in the art, literature, and soft Tuscan light of this beautiful city. The city of Dante and *David,* Machiavelli and the Medicis, Guccis, and Puccis is still the perfect place to fall in love all over again.

The food in Florence is simple and hearty, without rich sauces or elaborate spices. The cuisine reflects the Tuscan emphasis on bread, beans, deep green extra-virgin olive oil, wild game, free-range poultry, and grilled and roasted meats. Florentine restaurants are not gourmet, but many dishes are prepared so well that the food is considered to be some of the best in Italy. Because of the influx of almost one million visitors a year, the good-value restaurants are known to visitors as well as natives. To avoid eating with your fellow compatriots, plan to eat dinner when the Italians do, after 8:30 or 9:00 P.M.

In Florence you will probably eat more bread than you will pasta. Most of the bread is baked without salt, which seems odd at first, but the contrast between salty *prosciutto* and plain unsalted bread is almost addictive. Stale bread goes into some of their best dishes. *Crostini* (toasted bread spread with chicken liver pâté) and *fettunta* (a piece of day-old bread toasted and rubbed with garlic and soaked in olive oil) are delicious *antipasti. Ribollita,* a hearty vegetable soup with beans and black cabbage, reheated and poured over a thick slice of bread, is a favorite first course. In the summer, *panzanella* (a salad of torn bread tossed with tomatoes and onion in red wine and virgin olive oil) and *pappardelle* (rich egg pasta sauced with *porcini* mushrooms) are dishes to remember. Meat courses delight all carnivores, especially the *bistecca alla fiorentina,* a two- to three-inch slab of Chianti beef, salted and coated with olive oil and grilled juicy rare. Chianti wine in a straw-covered bottle is a fit accompaniment to any meal. For an even better wine, look for Chianti Classico, with the *gallo nero*, or black rooster, label on the neck.

Dessert is usually a piece of fresh fruit or a glass of *vin santo*, a sweet wine made from dried grapes, drunk with a plateful of *cantuccini di Prato* (also called *biscotti di Prato*), hard almond cookies, dipped into the wine. It is a light and very nice finish to any Tuscan meal.

Note: The street numbers of commercial establishments (stores, restaurants, and businesses) are indicated by a red "r" in the address. A blue or black "b" means that the address is a hotel or residence. To add to the fun, addresses are seldom in sequence as we think they should be; instead they are in sequence according to the "r" or the "b" in the address. In other words, the "r" numbers follow sequence and so do the "b" numbers, but they are not necessarily next to one another, which is confusing to the unknowing foreigner.

RESTAURANTS IN FLORENCE

Acquacotta	24
Alimentari	30
Almanacco (Centro Vegetariano Fiorentino)	32
Antica Trattoria e Fiaschetteria	40
Antichi Cancelli	33
Armando	30
Baccus	31
Bar Ricchi	40
Bar/Trattoria Santa Croce	46
Belle Donne	25
Buca dell'Orafo	44
Cafaggi	33
Caffè Caruso	54
Cantinetta Antinori	25
CarLie's	47
Croce al Trebbio	25
Da Benvenuto	48
Da Giorgio	51
Da Pennello	27
Fiaschetteria al Panino	48
Gastronomia Vera	41
I' Cchè C'é C'é	55
Il Barroccio	49
Il Cardellino	34

Il Contadino   51
Il Fornaio   45
Il Granduca   28
Il Triangolo delle Bermude   52
I Raddi   42
La Falterona   35
La Lampara   52
La Macelleria   35
Le Mossacce   28
Le Sorelle   24
Montecatini   55
Osteria del Cinghiale Bianco   45
Palle d'Oro   29
Pasticceria Marino   42
Ristorante de' Medici   53
Taverna del Bronzino   36
Trattoria Casalinga   43
Trattoria da Tito   23
Trattoria del Carmine   43
Trattoria Enzo e Piero   37
Trattoria Gozzi   37
Trattoria Guelfa   53
Trattoria Mario   38
Trattoria Zà Zà   39
Vini del Chianti   29
Vivoli   50

MISCELLANEOUS LOCATIONS IN FLORENCE

PIAZZA DELLA LIBERTÀ
Trattoria da Tito

PIAZZALE MICHELANGELO
Le Sorelle

PIAZZA S. AMBROGIO
Acquacotta

Trattoria da Tito
via San Gallo, 112r

Trattoria da Tito is an undiscovered jewel far from the usual tourist beat, and that is why it is so good. (Until now no one knew about it, and you won't tell anyone, will you?) I like Tito because it is so typically Tuscan, complete with yellowing walls lined with photos of dubious value, quick and friendly service, and reasonable prices for food of uncompromisingly good quality.

At lunchtime you will need a shoehorn to get in, because the place is so packed with the regulars who have made this their neighborhood command post. Cheap Eaters will like the all-inclusive *menù turistico*, but I recommend loosening the money belt a notch or two and ordering from the *piatti del giorno* (daily-special menu). Carbohydrate fans will have a field day with the long list of authentic pastas and rice dishes. The *ribollita* (vegetable and bean soup), ravioli with spinach and Gorgonzola cheese, and the *pappardelle alle salsiccia e funghi* (broad noodles with sausage and mushrooms) are especially good. Carnivores can choose from a range of top-quality meats, and fish-eaters will love the grilled salmon or baked sole. In the event that there is room for dessert, try the *dolce della casa* (the special house dessert of the day) or an assortment of Tuscan cheeses.

AREA
piazza della Libertà

TELEPHONE
47.24.75

OPEN
Mon–Fri lunch and dinner, Sat lunch

CLOSED
Sat dinner; Sun; Aug 10–31

HOURS
Lunch noon–3 P.M., dinner 7–10:30 P.M.

RESERVATIONS
Advised

CREDIT CARDS
MC, V

À LA CARTE
L 38,000, beverage not included

MENÙ TURISTICO
L 20,000, 3 courses, beverage included

ENGLISH
Yes

COVER & SERVICE CHARGES
L 1,500 cover, 10% service charge

Le Sorelle
via San Niccolò, 30r

AREA
Near piazzale Michelangelo
TELEPHONE
23.42.722
OPEN
Fri-Wed lunch and dinner
CLOSED
Thurs; 1 week in summer
(varies)
HOURS
Lunch noon–2:30 P.M.,
dinner 7:30–10:30 P.M.
RESERVATIONS
Sun lunch
CREDIT CARDS
AMEX, DC, MC, V
À LA CARTE
L 26,000, beverage not
included
MENÙ TURISTICO
None
ENGLISH
Yes
COVER & SERVICE CHARGES
Included

Italian families traditionally gather the clan together for Sunday lunch, which is usually a long, drawn-out affair where the men listen to the soccer game, the women compare household and child-raising tips, and everyone eats and drinks a little too much. A good place for cost-conscious visitors to witness this weekly ritual is at Le Sorelle, on a nondescript street across the Arno from all the action. There won't be another tourist in sight—at least until you have finished reading this.

The food is remarkably good, despite harried service by overworked waiters zipping by in Levis and tennis shoes. The price of the meal includes the cover and service charges and the garnishes for the second course, which is enough to make all Cheap Eaters take serious notice. The menu changes weekly and everything is made here, including indulgent desserts and interesting pastas. If you go in the late winter, you will find fat tube pasta covered with sausage and mushrooms, and polenta mixed with Tuscan cheese, as eye-opening first courses. Second plates include fat asparagus topped with a fried egg; snails stewed in a red wine, tomato, and garlic sauce; and *baccalà con porri:* dried salt cod fried with leeks. When dessert time rolls around, plan to repent later and order the apple torte or the ever-popular *tiramisù.*

Acquacotta
via dei Pilastri, 51r

AREA
piazza S. Ambrogio
TELEPHONE
24.29.07
OPEN
Thurs–Mon lunch and dinner,
Tues lunch
CLOSED
Tues dinner; Wed; Aug
HOURS
Lunch noon–2 P.M., dinner
7:30–10 P.M.

When I visited the Paperback Exchange (see *Cheap Sleeps in Italy*), run by American Emily Rosner and her Italian husband Maurizio Panichi, they told me about their favorite trattoria in the neighborhood: Acquacotta. I tried it several times and I always liked it because the interior, the waiters, the wine, and the food were all reliably Tuscan. The three-room operation is served by a corps of waiters wearing long white aprons, with black vests in the winter. Each room is attractive, but I prefer sitting at a table in the main room where I can see the chefs at work in the kitchen.

Whatever you order will be good and well prepared. The house specialty is *acquacotta,* a rich vegetable soup served over toasted bread and topped with a poached egg. Budgeteers will go for the grilled chicken, pork chops, or veal scaloppine with lemon. Those willing to step out a bit more can consider the delicious *bollito misto e salsa verde,* or boiled pigs' feet, tongue, and breast served with pesto sauce. Try it—you will be as pleasantly surprised as I was. Desserts do not quite live up to expectations, but if you want a little something, the lemon sorbet or fresh fruit makes a good finish.

RESERVATIONS
Not necessary
CREDIT CARDS
None
À LA CARTE
L 28,000, beverage not included
MENÙ TURISTICO
None
ENGLISH
Yes
COVER & SERVICE CHARGES
L 2,000 cover, no service charge
MISCELLANEOUS
The address of the Paperback Exchange is via Fiesolana, 31r; tel: 24.78.154

RESTAURANTS NEAR IL DUOMO

Belle Donne
Cantinetta Antinori
Croce al Trebbio
Da Pennello
Il Granduca
Le Mossacce
Palle d'Oro
Vini del Chianti

Belle Donne
via delle Belle Donne, 16r

There is no sign or menu outside the Belle Donne, only a cluster of Florentines waiting for a vacant seat. The inside is dominated by a massive fruit and vegetable display and a forest of green plants. The closely spaced marble-topped tables for two or four, and the banquette benches around the walls with low-to-the-ground green stools, are filled to capacity. The menu is written on a blackboard and is never the same two days in a row. You can eat lightly and order just one course, or go full tilt and have everything from soup to dessert if you are starved. If they are available, don't pass up the cream of chestnut soup or the avocado and zucchini salad. For the second course, look for chicken in lemon, or Carpaccio (thinly sliced raw beef filet) served with a salad of bitter greens. My favorite veg-

AREA
Il Duomo
TELEPHONE
23.82.609
OPEN
Mon–Fri lunch and dinner
CLOSED
Sat; Sun; Aug
HOURS
Lunch 12:30–2:30 P.M., dinner 7:30–9:30 P.M.
RESERVATIONS
Advised
CREDIT CARDS
None
À LA CARTE
L 18,000–20,000, beverage not included
MENÙ TURISTICO
None

ENGLISH
Yes
COVER & SERVICE CHARGES
L 1,000 cover; 10% service
charge

etable is the fennel gratin, and for dessert, the custard is light as a cloud. The service tends to be rushed and borders on the rude, especially during the peak lunch hour. Don't let this deter you—it doesn't the locals and it shouldn't you.

Cantinetta Antinori
Palazzo Antinori, piazza Antinori, 3r

AREA
Il Duomo
TELEPHONE
29.22.34, 23.59.827
OPEN
Mon–Fri lunch and dinner
CLOSED
Sat; Sun; Aug
HOURS
Lunch 12:30–2:30 P.M., dinner
7–10:30 P.M.
RESERVATIONS
Essential
CREDIT CARDS
AMEX, DC, MC, V
À LA CARTE
L 50,000, 3 courses and dessert,
beverage not included;
L 15,000, salad and sandwich
and wine
MENÙ TURISTICO
None
ENGLISH
Yes
COVER & SERVICE CHARGES
L 4,000 cover,
10% service charge

Many years ago, owners of famous estates around Florence sold wine and other products of their land from the cellars of their palaces in town. Following this longstanding tradition, the Antinori family has established the Cantinetta in their fifteenth-century Renaissance Palazzo Antinori in the heart of Florence. Without question, this is a magnificent showplace for the vintages of the oldest and most distinguished wine producer in Tuscany. The dark-paneled bar and restaurant always are filled with beautifully clad Florentines who have made this the most popular wine bar in the city. All of the food comes from the family estates, which are known especially for their rich extra-virgin olive oil, outstanding cheeses, and fine wines. Full meals can run into the Big Splurge category—and are worth every delicious bite. If you want to spend less and still enjoy this memorable experience, you can sample a sandwich, a salad, or perhaps a plate of assorted cheeses, along with a glass or two of one of their excellent wines or champagnes.

Croce al Trebbio
via delle Belle Donne, 47–49r

AREA
Il Duomo and piazza Santa
Maria Novella
TELEPHONE
28.70.89
OPEN
Tues–Sun lunch and dinner
CLOSED
Mon; NAC
HOURS
Lunch noon–2:30 P.M.,
dinner 7–10 P.M.

A meal at Croce al Trebbio is pleasant and unhurried, with good service and food to match. The interior is upmarket rustic, with beams, bountiful food displays, and two walls papered with foreign money. The downstairs basement features a 100-year-old brick arched ceiling and rough stone walls. If romance is on your agenda, this is a more intimate place to dine, especially in the evening when the lights are low.

Newcomers and oldtimers alike go for either the *menù turistico* or the daily specials. The à la carte choices are broader, but they are only borderline bargains. The meal gets off to a stunning start if you order the *bresaola rucola e parmigiano*: dried beef with arugula and paper-thin slices of fresh Parmesan cheese. First-course standouts include a creamy rice dish filled with fresh shrimp, and an especially worthy *pasta e fagioli*: pasta in a broth of beans with onions, bacon, and tomato, sprinkled with grated cheese. The down-to-earth dish of tomatoes and potatoes cooked with salt cod, and the *seppie con piselli* (squid with peas) are unusual main courses worth serious thought. Inexpensive house wines complement the meal perfectly. Desserts are decidedly limited, so there is no use to plan on having one unless you must finish with some sweet tidbit.

RESERVATIONS
Advised for dinner

CREDIT CARDS
MC, V

À LA CARTE
L 35,000, beverage not included

MENÙ TURISTICO
L 18,000, 3 courses, beverages included

ENGLISH
Yes

COVER & SERVICE CHARGES
L 2,000 cover, service included

Da Pennello
via Dante Alighieri, 4r

Da Pennello has been discovered, but never mind—the brightly lit restaurant with its pretty garden for summer dining is deservedly popular with both Italians and visitors to Florence. It is located on a narrow street near Dante's house, about a five-minute stroll from Il Duomo in the direction of the Uffizi Gallery and the Arno River. The chef is widely known for producing an impressive variety of outstanding *antipasti*, and, if you wish, you can make an entire meal out of these wonderful hors d'oeuvres.

The two *menù turistichi* (set-price menus) offer good Cheap Eating. The first, at L 22,000, consists of a choice of *primi piatti* (first courses) of several pastas or the soup of the day, and *secondi piatti* (second courses) of roast loin of pork or beef, veal scaloppine, or an omelette, along with vegetables or a salad and dessert. Wine is extra. For five thousand lire more, you get multiple trips to the *antipasti* table, in addition to everything else.

The restaurant is always packed to the walls, so if you arrive without reservations, be prepared to wait up to one hour.

AREA
Il Duomo

TELEPHONE
29.48.48

OPEN
Tues–Fri lunch and dinner, Sun lunch

CLOSED
Mon; Sun dinner; first 3 weeks in Aug; 1 week between Christmas and New Year's

HOURS
Lunch noon–2:30 P.M., dinner 7–10 P.M.

RESERVATIONS
Definitely

CREDIT CARDS
None

À LA CARTE
L 30,000, beverage included

MENÙ TURISTICO
L 22,000 and L 27,000, beverage not included

ENGLISH
Yes

COVER & SERVICE CHARGES
L 2,000 cover, no service charge

Il Granduca
via dei Calzaiuoli, 57r

AREA
Il Duomo
TELEPHONE
29.81.12
OPEN
Thurs–Tues
CLOSED
Wed; NAC
HOURS
10 A.M.–midnight
RESERVATIONS
Not accepted
CREDIT CARDS
None
À LA CARTE
Prices start at L 2,000
MENÙ TURISTICO
None
ENGLISH
Enough
COVER & SERVICE CHARGES
None

For the scoop on some of the best *gelati* in Florence, don't forget Il Granduca near Il Duomo and piazza della Repubblica. Here you will have some difficult decisions: fresh kiwi, strawberry, melon, pineapple, papaya, blackberry, coffee custard, or mint ice cream. Or, will it be a dish of chocolate *semifreddo*, that dairy-based *gelato* fluffed with cream to a mousse-like texture and topped with a cloud of whipped cream? Warning: *Semifreddo* is very fragile and made only during the cooler months. If you are here in the heat of August, it won't be an option. For dieters, there are four sugar-free flavors and a few frozen yogurts. For kids of all shapes and ages, cones come plain, chocolate, and nut-dipped. Prices start at L 2,000 for a scoop in a cup and go on to L 15,000 for a gargantuan blitz.

Le Mossacce
via del Proconsolo, 55r

AREA
Between Il Duomo and the
Bargello
TELEPHONE
29.43.61
OPEN
Mon–Fri lunch and dinner
CLOSED
Sat; Sun; Aug
HOURS
Lunch noon–2:30 P.M., dinner
7–9:30 P.M.
RESERVATIONS
Not accepted; go early for best
results
CREDIT CARDS
AMEX, MC, V
À LA CARTE
L 24,000, beverage not included
MENÙ TURISTICO
L 20,000, 2 courses and
beverage, no dessert
ENGLISH
Yes
COVER & SERVICE CHARGES
L 2,000 cover, service included

Le Mossacce, midway between the Bargello and Il Duomo, is a very convenient choice for anyone visiting these two must-sees in Florence. At lunch, the scene is chaotic, to say the least. Habitués pack the century-old restaurant, where animated seating is at miniscule wooden tables set with white linen napkins and paper place mats.

Le Mossacce is known as a sanctuary of earthy Tuscan cooking, with few concessions to any cuisine outside the region. Here you feast on *ribollita* or minestrone, *cannelloni*, boiled beef with pesto, roast veal, and the dream of all beef eaters, *bistecca alla fiorentina*. Dessert choices are limited to fresh fruit, *biscotti* dipped in sweet wine, crème caramel, and cream-filled puff pastry. House wines are modestly priced and the *menù turistico* a buy, even though dessert is extra. English is spoken and the menu is translated, so eating here is never stressful if your Italian leaves something to be desired.

Palle d'Oro
via Sant'Antonio 43–43r

For a satisfying lunch or light dinner, this budget destination is a Cheap Eat find on an interesting shopping street midway between Il Duomo and the big central market. You can join the well-dressed crowd ordering freshly crafted sandwiches up front, or take a seat at one of the tables in back for a brimming bowl of soup or pasta, a fragrantly roasted chicken with a green salad, or a piece of grilled salmon seasoned with fresh lemon and a splash of olive oil.

This antiseptically clean spot is slightly surgical in decor, reminding me of a fifties coffee shop, with wooden booths and tables. Don't let this turn you off, because it is always dependable for good, fast food *alla italiano*, and we all need something like this to fall back on no matter where we are.

AREA
Il Duomo and piazza Mercato Centrale

TELEPHONE
28.83.83

OPEN
Mon–Sat lunch and dinner

CLOSED
Sun; Aug

HOURS
Lunch noon–2:30 P.M., dinner 7:30–11 P.M.

RESERVATIONS
Not accepted

CREDIT CARDS
MC, V

À LA CARTE
L 10,000, beverage included

MENÙ TURISTICO
None

ENGLISH
Enough

COVER & SERVICE CHARGES
L 2,000 cover, no service charge

Vini del Chianti
via dei Cimatori (no number)

One of the best ways to cut food costs and have good Cheap Eats in the bargain is to have lunch at a snack bar. Here you will be joined by savvy Italians who know that they can have the chef's special, a sandwich, a bowl of pasta, or a salad for a mere fraction of the cost of a restaurant meal. Further savings are possible if the meal is eaten while standing rather than seated at a table. Only you can decide how far you want to pinch your lire on that score.

This brings me to Vini del Chianti, a stand-up wine bar and sandwich counter where you can order freshly prepared sandwiches to eat there or have packaged to go. They serve only sandwiches and specialize in those made with *prosciutto crudo*—air-dried, salt-cured ham—and homemade chicken liver pâté spread on thinly sliced bread. Vegetarians will love their sandwich loaded with onions, artichokes, stewed peppers, and mozzarella cheese. With a glass of Chianti Classico or a light Tuscan white, you will have a satisfying Cheap Eat with enough lire left over to enjoy a nice dinner later on.

AREA
Il Duomo

TELEPHONE
None

OPEN
Mon–Sat

CLOSED
Sun; dinner; 15 days in Aug (varies)

HOURS
Wine bar open 8 A.M.–8 P.M.; continuous service

RESERVATIONS
Not accepted

CREDIT CARDS
None

À LA CARTE
L 500, bread with pâté; L 2,500 and up for other sandwiches

MENÙ TURISTICO
None

ENGLISH
Limited

COVER & SERVICE CHARGES
None

Alimentari
Armando
Baccus

Alimentari
via Parione, 12r

AREA
piazza Goldoni
TELEPHONE
21.40.67
OPEN
Mon–Sat lunch
CLOSED
Wed from 3 P.M. on; Sun; Aug
HOURS
Food store 8 A.M.–3 P.M., 5–7:30 P.M.; lunch noon–3 P.M., sandwiches anytime
RESERVATIONS
Not accepted
CREDIT CARDS
None
À LA CARTE
L 3,500–6,000, beverage not included
MENÙ TURISTICO
None
ENGLISH
Enough
COVER & SERVICE CHARGES
None

My favorite place for a wonderful sandwich stacked with prosciutto, fresh buffalo-milk mozzarella cheese, and thinly sliced tomatoes is Alimentari near piazza Goldoni. This fancy-food store sells designer sandwiches as fast as they can spread them, as well as delicious hot and cold dishes to lunch audiences from Monday through Saturday. To avoid the ten-deep lunch crunch waiting in line, go before 1 P.M., when the stores and offices in the neighborhood let out for the lunch break. If you are lucky, you will snag a seat at one of the five or six upside-down barrels in the center of the room. Otherwise, you can stand at the bar with the rest of the crowd and down a glass of Chianti with your repast.

This is also a fine place to keep in mind if you are putting together a picnic lunch, or want to buy something to take back to your hotel for later.

Armando
borgo Ognissanti, 140r

AREA
piazza Goldoni
TELEPHONE
21.62.19
OPEN
Thurs–Tues
CLOSED
Tues dinner; Wed; Aug
HOURS
Lunch 12:30–2:30 P.M., dinner 7:30–10 P.M.
RESERVATIONS
Advised, especially for dinner
CREDIT CARDS
MC, V
À LA CARTE
L 28,000, beverage not included

Before I left on my trip to Italy to do the research for this book and the companion volume, *Cheap Sleeps in Italy,* many people told me not to miss Armando's, a typical Tuscan trattoria serving very good food in an ever-crowded, cheerful atmosphere. After trying it, I share their enthusiasm and can wholeheartedly put it on my short list of best-for-value restaurants in Florence offering cooking that will not only please, but nourish us all very well. The service could not be more friendly, and the staff is multilingual, as is the menu. The ambience is as authentic as the cuisine. As the evening wears on, it can get loud, but that is part of the fun of eating at Armando's. Keep in mind that Italians dine late; in fact, at

9:30 P.M. they are still milling about waiting to be seated.

The winning vote for the best pasta dish goes to the *ravioli al burro e salvia,* homemade ravioli stuffed with ricotta cheese and sage with a buttery sauce over it. Throw cholesterol and fat worries to the wind for just one night and treat yourself to this exceptional dish. Another hands-down favorite in the pasta department goes to the *spaghetti alla carrettiera,* homemade pasta with a spicy sauce made from garlic, fresh basil, tomato, and red pepper. This dish will wake up your taste buds for sure. Even if you have spent a lifetime turning up your nose at liver, please reconsider it here and try the *fegato alla salvia,* calves' liver broiled just to the tender pink stage. In the dessert department, nothing is a knockout, so opt for an assortment of local cheeses, a scoop of cool gelato, or, better yet, save those calories for another opportunity.

Baccus
via Borgo Ognissanti

Pastas, pizzas, hamburgers, huge salads, and incredible ice cream desserts stream out of the Baccus kitchen to a young and trendy crowd with healthy appetites and hearty voices. All of this in an avant-garde setting with mirrors, booths, hanging lights, and a noise level that ranges from a moderate din to "Say that again, I can't hear you."

Thank goodness the twelve-page menu is translated into English. It starts with drinks and appetizers, moves on to innovative salads, pages of daily pastas that include all the tried-and-true combinations, plus some that might make you wonder. For instance, the *penne natale 85* mixes mushrooms, salmon, vodka, and cream, the *risotto Middle East* combines heart of palm, pineapple, and cream; while the *tagliolini tropicali* is topped with shrimp, curry, and kiwis. Sometimes there is just no accounting for taste! If the pastas do not appeal, maybe the hamburger Baccus will. It is a juicy burger covered with mushrooms and melted cheese. Rounding out the menu are *crostini,*

MENÙ TURISTICO
None

ENGLISH
Yes

COVER & SERVICE CHARGES
L 2,500 cover, 10% service charge

AREA
piazza Goldoni

TELEPHONE
28.37.14

OPEN
Mon–Sat lunch and dinner

CLOSED
Sun; 1–15 Aug

HOURS
Lunch 12:30–2:30 P.M., dinner 7 P.M.–1:00 A.M.

RESERVATIONS
Advised at night

CREDIT CARDS
AMEX, MC, V

À LA CARTE
L 20,000, beverage not included

MENÙ TURISTICO
None

ENGLISH
Yes

COVER & SERVICE CHARGES
L 1,000 cover for lunch, L 2,000 cover for dinner, no service charge for either

pizzas, calzone (those wonderful stuffed pizzas) and fabulous *focaccia* bread with everything from tuna to smoked salmon and artichokes. Ice cream reigns supreme for dessert, with more than fourteen possibilities ranging from a banana split with hot chocolate to a mere scoop of plain strawberry.

RESTAURANTS NEAR THE PIAZZA MERCATO CENTRALE

Almanacco (Centro Vegetariano Fiorentino)
Antichi Cancelli
Cafaggi
Il Cardellino
La Falterona
La Macelleria
Taverna del Bronzino
Trattoria Enzo e Piero
Trattoria Gozzi
Trattoria Mario
Trattoria Zà Zà

Almanacco (Centro Vegetariano Fiorentino)
via delle Ruote, 30r

AREA
piazza della Indipendenza and piazza Mercato Centrale

TELEPHONE
47.50.30

OPEN
Tues–Fri lunch and dinner, Sat and Sun dinner

CLOSED
Sat and Sun lunch; Mon; Aug

HOURS
Lunch 1–2:30 P.M., dinner 7:30–10:30 P.M.

RESERVATIONS
Not accepted

CREDIT CARDS
None

À LA CARTE
L 10,000, beverage not included

MENÙ TURISTICO
None

If you are a first-time diner at Almanacco, you will be required to pay a one-time L 10,000 fee. You will then be eligible to return as often as you like and also will receive discounts on some of their programs and film showings. The exceptional vegetarian food is served in a warm and friendly atmosphere and is dished out cafeteria style to the many faithful diners who eat here with great regularity. The menu changes every day and varies with the seasons. As you enter the restaurant, look at the printed blackboard, decide what you want, write it down on the form provided, and take it to the cashier and pay. Then go to the kitchen, give them your menu form, and they will ladle out your portion. You then take your food to a communal table either in the smoking or nonsmoking room. The varied selection of food usually includes rice and pasta dishes, casseroles made from beans and legumes, quiches, soufflés, and great composed salads. Desserts fall into the lead-ball category, and I recommend skipping them.

Note: There is no sign outside the restaurant. Look for the round sign with a red telephone receiver hanging above the entrance at via delle Ruote, 30. This is it.

Antichi Cancelli
via Faenza, 73r

Trattoria Antichi Cancelli, which means "the old gate," is under the same ownership as Trattoria Guelfa (see page 53). With its hanging peppers and garlic braids, potted plants, and tiny paper-covered marble-topped tables set under a brick ceiling, it looks like something from a film set. The difference, of course, is the great food and jovial ambience. It doesn't take newcomers long to blend in and to quickly catch the mood of the place. As with Trattoria Guelfa, do not even *think* of arriving without reservations, and even then you can count on having to wedge yourself into the crowd and wait for a table.

It is important that you come prepared to eat. Management takes a dim view of dieters or anyone else not ordering at least a pasta, main course, and dessert. The daily menu is based on what is best at the market during each season. The dishes of Tuscany are well prepared, and everything from the *antipasti* and pasta to the sauces and desserts is made here. The filling portions promise that no one will be thinking about the next meal for a long time.

Cafaggi
via Guelfa, 35r

One of the best ways to find good Cheap Eats is to ask the natives where they go. The top contender on via Guelfa, between piazza della Indipendenza and piazza San Marco off via Cavour, is Cafaggi. This plain-Jane restaurant has been in the same family for six decades. It consists of two rooms done in boring beige. The second room off the kitchen is slightly more appealing due to a few plants and flowers on

ENGLISH
Yes

COVER & SERVICE CHARGES
L 2,000 cover, no service charge

MISCELLANEOUS
One-time L 10,000 membership fee required

AREA
piazza Mercato Centrale

TELEPHONE
21.89.27

OPEN
Tues–Sun lunch and dinner

CLOSED
Mon; NAC

HOURS
Lunch noon–2:30 P.M., dinner 7–10:30 P.M.

RESERVATIONS
Absolutely essential

CREDIT CARDS
AMEX, DC, MC, V

À LA CARTE
L 30,000, beverage not included

MENÙ TURISTICO
L 18,000 and L 20,000, 3 courses, wine and coffee included

ENGLISH
Yes

COVER & SERVICE CHARGES
L 2,000 cover, 10% service charge

AREA
piazza Mercato Centrale

TELEPHONE
29.49.89

OPEN
Tues–Sat lunch and dinner, Sun lunch

CLOSED
Sun dinner; Mon; Aug

HOURS
Lunch noon–2:30 P.M.,
dinner 7–10 P.M.

RESERVATIONS
Advised for dinner, weekends,
and holidays

CREDIT CARDS
None

À LA CARTE
L 35,000–40,000, beverage not
included

MENÙ TURISTICO
L 25,000, 3 courses, beverage
included; *menù vegetariano*:
L 22,000, 2 courses, beverage
included; *menù leggero*:
L 24,000, 2 courses, beverage
included

ENGLISH
Yes

COVER & SERVICE CHARGES
L 2,500 cover, 12% service
charge

each table. You must remember that the reason for being here is to dine, not to lounge in magnificent surroundings. After you have been served and tasted the fine food, you will quickly forget all about the dull atmosphere.

Cheap Eaters *must* stay with one of the set-priced menus, either the three-course *menù turistico*, which includes several choices of pasta, meat, dessert, and beverage; the *menù vegetariano*; or the *menù leggero*, the dieter's menu. These last two have limited selections, but include either wine or mineral water. If you stray onto the à la carte side of things, you will not have a Cheap Eat at all.

The chef prides himself on turning out carefully prepared dishes using the freshest seasonal ingredients. Good bets include any of the pasta or rice dishes, veal in buttery asparagus sauce, any of the fresh fish, and, for dessert, an exceptional cream caramel or soft ice cream with espresso. The house wine is adequate, so there is no need to splurge on anything better unless you want to.

Il Cardellino
via San Gallo, 37r

AREA
piazza San Marco and piazza
Mercato Centrale

TELEPHONE
47.50.90

OPEN
Wed–Mon lunch and dinner

CLOSED
Tues; 10–31 Aug

HOURS
Lunch noon–3 P.M.,
dinner 7–10:30 P.M.

RESERVATIONS
Essential at night

CREDIT CARDS
AMEX, DC, MC, V

À LA CARTE
L 28,000 beverage not included

MENÙ TURISTICO
L 18,000, includes all courses,
beverage included

I found Il Cardellino because it was just two blocks from my flat in Florence. Each day as I walked by, I saw neighborhood locals filling the place and thought, these people must be on to something good. Naturally I had to try it, and when I did I found food made for seriously good eating: subtly flavored pastas, quality meats, and fresh salads priced within reason and served with good cheer.

Tops on the menu are the specials, which the chef changes every two weeks. If it is available when you are here, start with the *spaghetti alla carrettiera*, which has a rich tomato sauce highlighted with red peppers. The roasted chicken is wonderfully moist inside, with perfectly crisp skin, but is served with French fries that are soggy and tasteless. Ask to have it accompanied with a fresh vegetable or a salad instead. For an unusual dessert, look for the *fritelle alla fiorentina*, deep-fried rice-flour dumplings studded with dried fruits. They sound heavy as lead, but they are feather-light and almost melt in your mouth. If you order the house wine, the white is better than the rough red.

ENGLISH
Some

COVER & SERVICE CHARGES
L 2,500 cover, 12% service charge

La Falterona
via San Zanobi, 10r

For authentic blue collar atmosphere near the piazza Mercato Centrale, eat at La Falterona, a family-run trattoria that has been serving market workers since time began. The decor consists of coats hanging from hooks around the room, a faded map of Florence on one wall, a calendar and unframed curling posters on another, and ancient waiters serving stout, red-faced diners. For the fullest effect, sit in the front room, where you can keep an eye on all the goings-on.

No one pretends here. Originality is not a virtue, and parsley is not on anyone's shopping list. This is a real neighborhood restaurant: small, with basic wholesome food that has absolutely no frills or surprises. The low-priced *menù turistico* attracts a crowd because it includes three courses and all the Chianti you can drink. The meat dishes are good, especially the chicken in white wine, the roast veal, and the overwhelming *bistecca alla fiorentina*, which sells for 1,000 lire less per gram than any other place in the city.

AREA
piazza Mercato Centrale
TELEPHONE
21.61.12
OPEN
Thurs–Tues lunch and dinner
CLOSED
Wed; July
HOURS
Lunch noon–2:30 P.M., dinner 7–9 P.M.
RESERVATIONS
Not accepted
CREDIT CARDS
None
À LA CARTE
L 20,000, beverage not included
MENÙ TURISTICO
L 18,000, 3 courses, beverage included
ENGLISH
Yes
COVER & SERVICE CHARGES
L 2,000 cover, no service

La Macelleria
via San Zanobi, 97r

In its past life, La Macelleria was a corner butcher shop. About ten years ago, a young couple named Danielle and Daniello bought it and turned it into a high-stepping *ristorante* that is now a favored rendez-vous for the neighborhood. In the transformation from butcher shop to eating place, the owners kept the original marble-topped butcher counters and walls. They put in black-and-white tiled tables and green padded chairs; covered the walls with paintings, photos, and drawings of animals; placed bouquets of fresh and dried flowers everywhere; and added a mezzanine to the second room, where you will find a bookshelf

AREA
piazza Mercato Centrale (15-minute walk)
TELEPHONE
48.62.44
OPEN
Mon–Fri lunch and dinner, Sat dinner
CLOSED
Sat lunch; Sun; Aug
HOURS
Lunch 12:30–3 P.M., dinner 7–10 P.M.
RESERVATIONS
Advised

CREDIT CARDS
AMEX, MC, V

À LA CARTE
L 25,000, beverage not
included

MENÙ TURISTICO
L 20,000, 3 courses, beverage
not included

ENGLISH
Yes

COVER & SERVICE CHARGES
L 1,500 cover,
10% service charge

with magazines and books in case you want to brush up on your Italian. Admittedly, La Macelleria is out of the way, but that is a big part of its charm, because you rarely see anyone but Italians eating here.

Daniello is a talented chef who creates wonderful Tuscan fare for an appreciative public impressed by the lofty standards he maintains in his kitchen. The *almost*-legible handwritten menu concentrates on beef, veal, lamb, and chicken, with interesting specials and first-class desserts. Dishes I hope to try again include the *gnocchetti tricolore* (three types of *gnocchi* flavored with ginger, curry, and chives), a soul-warming beef stew served with heavenly mashed potatoes, and a dessert crepe filled with whipped cream and slathered with chocolate sauce. Service can be slow, so don't plan on hurrying off to an early-afternoon appointment or an evening date. Just sit back, have another glass of wine, and enjoy being surrounded by attractive Italians who don't seem to have a care or a deadline in the world.

Taverna del Bronzino
via delle Ruote, 25r

AREA
piazza Mercato Centrale
(20-minute walk)

TELEPHONE
49.52.20

OPEN
Mon–Sat lunch and dinner

CLOSED
Sun; all holidays; Aug

HOURS
Lunch 12:30–2 P.M.,
dinner 7:30–10 P.M.

RESERVATIONS
Advised, especially for dinner
and a good table

CREDIT CARDS
AMEX, DC, MC, V

À LA CARTE
L 45,000, beverage not
included

MENÙ TURISTICO
None

Eating at the Taverna del Bronzino is always a great pleasure. It is a perfect place for big-splurge occasion dining, be it a birthday, an anniversary, or a romantic evening with the love of your life.

The interior is understated and elegant, with muted colors, flattering lighting, and comfortable seating at tables nicely appointed with crisp linens, heavy silver, and fresh flowers. Formally clad waiters offer graceful and unobtrusive service that is always one step ahead of what you need.

You are bound to be as impressed with the food as with the surroundings. It all starts with a glass of complimentary champagne and a plate of hors d'oeuvres to try while deciding what to order. If you want, your waiter will make knowledgeable suggestions to help you plan a meal around your specific likes. The imaginative dishes are inspired by the seasonal best of the Italian harvest. Fresh pasta is blanketed under robust sauces of tomato, basil, fresh seafood, and *funghi porcini*: flavorful wild mushrooms. Meat, poultry, and fish are perfectly cooked, gently perfumed with wines and fresh herbs. Sublime desserts and distinguished wines round out a meal you will fondly recall long after you have forgotten many others.

Trattoria Enzo e Piero
via Faenza, 105r

You can spot Enzo and Piero's trattoria by the stacks of wine kegs and bottles piled in front on the sidewalk. Inside, the dining room is very plain, with rough white stuccoed walls and lots of well-fed habitués sitting at red-linen-clad square tables. On each table is a bottle of Chianti wine vinegar and fine olive oil, so you can dress your own salad or, as the Italians do, sprinkle olive oil on just about everything but dessert.

Both Enzo and Piero are on hand each day to ensure that all runs well. They greet guests at the table, suggest what is best on the menu that day, and check back periodically to make sure everyone has everything needed. They also keep an eagle eye on the kitchen, where their high standards are reflected in absolutely fresh ingredients prepared with care. If you are here on a Friday, do try the *baccalà alla livornese*, salt cod cooked in a spicy red sauce with liberal doses of garlic. Other flavorful options are *tortellini alla cardinale*, with cream, tomatoes, and ham, and *osso buco*, veal shank cooked with carrots, tomatoes, onions, and a handful of herbs. The *menù turistico* is a Cheap Eat if there ever was one, even though it does not include the wine. For a few lire more, you can add a quarter or half carafe and still get away for under L 26,000 per person.

Trattoria Gozzi
piazza San Lorenzo, 8r

When in Florence, under no circumstances should you miss a trip to the Mercato Centrale de San

ENGLISH
Yes
COVER & SERVICE CHARGES
L 4,000 cover, no service charge
MISCELLANEOUS
Coat and tie recommended

AREA
piazza Mercato Centrale
TELEPHONE
21.49.01
OPEN
Mon–Fri most of year, Mon–Sat the rest
CLOSED
Sat and Sun in Feb, Mar, July, and Aug; 15–20 days mid-Aug
HOURS
Lunch noon–3 P.M., dinner 7–10 P.M.
RESERVATIONS
Advised for dinner
CREDIT CARDS
AMEX, DC, MC, V
À LA CARTE
L 28,000, beverage not included
MENÙ TURISTICO
L 18,000, 3 courses, beverage not included
ENGLISH
Yes
COVER & SERVICE CHARGES
L 2,500, no service charge

AREA
piazza Mercato Centrale

TELEPHONE	None
OPEN	Mon–Sat lunch only
CLOSED	Dinner; Sun, Aug
HOURS	Lunch noon–4 P.M.
RESERVATIONS	Not accepted
CREDIT CARDS	None
À LA CARTE	L 18,000–22,000, beverage included
MENÙ TURISTICO	None
ENGLISH	Some
COVER & SERVICE CHARGES	L 1,500 cover, no service charge

Lorenzo, a landmark nineteenth-century cast-iron building housing one of the largest and most interesting covered markets in Europe. On the outside of the market are hundreds of other stalls with sellers hawking everything from Florentine marbled paper goods and leather to jewelry, T-shirts, and silk scarves.

There are many places to eat around the market, some very good and others appallingly bad. One of the most authentic and tourist-free is Trattoria Gozzi, a true workingman's hangout, where you can taste hearty Tuscan food in two old-fashioned rooms filled with burly market men and their women. Everything is prepared fresh daily and, of course, changes with the seasons and availability at the market. You can count on chunky minestrone and bean soups, roasted meats, and sturdy boiled brisket. Good country bread and creamy desserts add to the pleasure of eating here. Follow the lead of fellow diners and order a bottle of Chianti to drink while enjoying the show, the friendly service, and a meal that will leave some extra lire in your pocket.

Trattoria Mario
via Rosina, 2r

AREA	piazza Mercato Centrale
TELEPHONE	21.85.50
OPEN	Mon–Sat, bar service and lunch
CLOSED	Dinner; Sun; Aug
HOURS	Bar service 7 A.M.–5 P.M., lunch noon–3 P.M.
RESERVATIONS	Not accepted
CREDIT CARDS	None
À LA CARTE	L 12,500, beverage not included

Whenever I am at the piazza Mercato Centrale and very hungry, I like to stop for lunch at Mario's and then spend an hour or so browsing through the stalls that ring the market.

The restaurant boasts an avid local crowd, all of whom seem to be on a first-name basis. Consequently, there is a great deal of good cheer and camaraderie as everyone sits around swapping lies and telling jokes. They all know to arrive early and order a glass or two of the house red while waiting for the lunch service to begin. Latecomers will have to wait or, worse yet, won't get their favorite dish, because the kitchen often runs out early.

The daily menu is posted on a board by the open kitchen. Friday is fish day, and on Thursday *gnocchi* is the dish to order. Other smart choices are the vegetable soup, stewed tripe, or a slab of roast veal or beef. You don't need to save room for dessert, because all they serve is fresh fruit or a glass of sweet wine with those wonderful hard almond-flavored dipping cookies. No coffee is served, either, but there are dozens of bars around the market. It is fun to merge with the crowd and stand at the bar for an after-lunch espresso that will recharge your batteries for the rest of the afternoon.

Trattoria Zà Zà
piazza Mercato Centrale, 26r

Trattoria Zà Zà, on the piazza Mercato Centrale, offers a winning mix of accommodating service, atmosphere, and hearty, enjoyable Tuscan food. Wooden picnic tables with long benches and hard stools line both the upstairs and downstairs dining areas. The walls are papered with film posters of Jimmy Cagney; Ingrid Bergman and Humphrey Bogart in the famous farewell scene in *Casablanca*; and Groucho Marx with his bushy black eyebrows and ever-present cigar. Overhead are three rows of shelves stacked high with the Chianti you will be drinking with your meal.

The wide-ranging menu offers a multitude of choices for every course. To start, order the trio of their best soups, which includes a bowl of *ribollita*, *pomodoro fresca* (fresh tomato), and *passato di fagioli con farro* (bean soup). The roast pork with beans, flavored with a hint of sage and extra-virgin olive oil, and the veal scaloppine with mushrooms are among the best entrées. The de rigueur dessert is Zà Zà's own *torta di mele alla Zà Zà*, an upside-down apple tart similar to the French *tarte Tatin*.

MENÙ TURISTICO
None

ENGLISH
Yes

COVER & SERVICE CHARGES
L 800 cover, no service charge

AREA
piazza Mercato Centrale

TELEPHONE
21.54.11

OPEN
Mon–Sat lunch and dinner

CLOSED
Sun; 1–24 Aug

HOURS
Lunch noon–2:30 P.M., dinner 7–10 P.M.

RESERVATIONS
Not necessary

CREDIT CARDS
AMEX, DC, MC, V

À LA CARTE
L 28,000, beverage not included

MENÙ TURISTICO
None

ENGLISH
Yes

COVER & SERVICE CHARGES
L 1,800 cover, no service charge

RESTAURANTS NEAR PIAZZA SANTO SPIRITO

Antica Trattoria e Fiaschetteria
Bar Ricchi
Gastronomia Vera
I Raddi
Pasticceria Marino
Trattoria Casalinga
Trattoria del Carmine

Antica Trattoria e Fiaschetteria
via Vellutini, 1r; angle via Toscanella

AREA
Pitti Palace and piazza
Santo Spirito
TELEPHONE
21.85.62
OPEN
Mon–Sat lunch and dinner
CLOSED
Sun; first half of Aug
HOURS
Lunch noon–2:30 P.M.,
dinner 7–9:30 P.M.
RESERVATIONS
Not accepted
CREDIT CARDS
None
À LA CARTE
L 12,000–15,000, beverage
included
MENÙ TURISTICO
None
ENGLISH
Limited
COVER & SERVICE CHARGES
L 1,500 cover, no service charge

If you are hell-bent on having Cheap Eats no matter what and do not mind a few frayed edges, you will be happy dining at Antica Trattoria e Fiaschetteria, a bare-bones restaurant where the same family has been serving the down-and-out for over forty years.

Regulars congregate in the first room, which has only four tables and a good view into the kitchen with its bubbling pots and the two grannies running the show. Families gravitate to the back room where nothing has been touched or spruced up for years, and probably never will be. The food is earthy and plentiful, but please don't expect *antipasti*, dessert, or coffee to be served because they are not available. You can expect, however, impressive portions of plain basics such as pasta with meat or tomato sauce; boiled, stewed, or roasted meats; a smattering of vegetables; and cheese or a piece of fresh fruit to finish. You will probably walk out for under 12,000 to 15,000 lire, including a quarter liter of country wine, and for Cheap Eaters who are not fussy, this is a good meal.

Bar Ricchi
piazza Santo Spirito, 9r

AREA
piazza Santo Spirito
TELEPHONE
21.58.64
OPEN
Mon–Sat lunch and bar service

What a pleasant surprise the Bar Ricchi turned out to be! I dashed in during a rainstorm to have a quick sandwich and warm myself with a strong espresso. Little did I know that the lunch served here has been gathering a growing set of fans for the past twelve years, and no wonder: the simple food is delicious. Yes, you can stand at the bar and order a sandwich, but I suggest sitting in the room next to the bar, which is lined with soft banquettes and tiny marble-topped café tables. Covering the walls here and in the bar is a fascinating display of framed photographs of Santo Spirito church. In the summer, plan to enjoy your lunch outside on the terrace, with its commanding view of the church.

The power of the kitchen is Alfonsina, the young wife of the owner of Bar Ricchi. Her menu selections are limited, but they change every day. When I was there she had rare roast beef with mashed potatoes, leg of lamb, and roast chicken. There are always daily pastas, a soup, and one or two seasonal vegetables. In the warmer months, beautiful salads and cold plates are on the menu. This is *not* the place to skip dessert. Either have a dish of fruit, or chocolate cream *gelato*, or indulge in one of Alfonsina's almost illegally rich pastries. As with most places like this, the best dishes go quickly, so plan to arrive early for lunch.

CLOSED
Sun; dinner; Aug 15–31

HOURS
Bar service 8 A.M.–8 P.M., lunch noon–2:30 P.M.

RESERVATIONS
Not accepted

CREDIT CARDS
AMEX, MC, V

À LA CARTE
L 6,000–8,000, beverage included

MENÙ TURISTICO
None

ENGLISH
Yes

COVER & SERVICE CHARGES
1,500 cover, no service charge

Gastronomia Vera
piazza Frescobaldi, 3r

Perfect picnics begin at Vera, one of the city's best-stocked and most appealing gourmet delicatessens. In addition to the usual roast meats, hanging hams and salamis, assorted cheeses, six types of olives, wines, homemade baked goods, olive oils, vinegars, and dairy products, Vera stocks over fifty dried pastas, countless dried herbs and spices, and enough fancy canned and bottled delicacies to keep you eating for weeks. Also available are mouthwatering soups and cold salads to go. Prices tend to be on the high side for almost everything, but for the unequalled quality of the food, I think it is well worth the extra outlay.

There are no tables for dining at Vera's, so plan to take whatever you order with you. Of course, this saves you the cover and service charges that would be added if you could eat your food here.

AREA
Across the River Arno, over the Ponte S. Trinità, en route to piazza Santo Spirito

TELEPHONE
21.54.65

OPEN
Mon-Sat

CLOSED
Wed afternoon; Sun; NAC

HOURS
Mon–Tues and Thurs–Sat 8:15 A.M.–8 P.M., Wed 8:15 A.M.–1:30 P.M.

RESERVATIONS
Not accepted

CREDIT CARDS
AMEX

À LA CARTE
Sandwiches start around L 4,000

MENÙ TURISTICO
None

ENGLISH
Yes

COVER & SERVICE CHARGES
None

I Raddi
via Ardiglione, 47r

AREA
piazza Santo Spirito and
Pitti Palace

TELEPHONE
21.10.72

OPEN
Mon–Sat

CLOSED
Mon lunch; Sun; Aug

HOURS
Lunch 12:30–2:30 P.M.,
dinner 7:30–10:30 P.M.

RESERVATIONS
Suggested for dinner

CREDIT CARDS
AMEX, MC, V

À LA CARTE
L 28,000, beverage not
included

MENÙ TURISTICO
None

ENGLISH
Yes

COVER & SERVICE CHARGES
L 2,000 cover, no service charge

Luciano Raddi, a former regional boxing champ, has switched careers. Now, with his wife and daughter, he cooks and serves home-style Florentine dishes in a trattoria somewhat off the usual tourist track, but close enough for a nice walk after lunch to the piazza Santo Spirito with its interesting church, or to the Pitti Palace a few blocks farther.

Quiet, well-spaced tables are set in a rough-hewn room dominated by a heavy-beamed ceiling. Art Nouveau pink tulip lights cast a soft evening glow in the large front room. The crowd at lunch is sparse, making it easy to get a good table without advance reservations. Things pick up at night, when the neighborhood pours in for an evening of conversation, good Chianti, and generous helpings of sensibly priced food. The menu does not go on forever, a sure sign that everything is fresh. For a good beginning, the *pasta primavera* with fresh tomatoes and basil is a light choice. Daily specials are always terrific, and if you enjoy tripe, liver, brains, or kidneys, they are exceptionally good here. Grilled meats, stews, and *bistecca alla fiorentina* round out the menu. The *dolce della casa*, either cheesecake or a lemon or chocolate pie, is made here, and everyone always saves room for at least a few bites.

Pasticceria Marino
piazza N. Sauro, 19r

AREA
piazza N. Sauro, en route to
piazza Santo Spirito

TELEPHONE
21.26.57

OPEN
Tues–Sun

CLOSED
Mon; Sun after 11 A.M.; Aug

HOURS
6:30 A.M.–8 P.M.

RESERVATIONS
Not accepted

CREDIT CARDS
None

For some of the best croissants (called *cornetti* or *brioche*) in Firenze, the name to remember is Pasticceria Marino, a bar and pastry shop on the piazza N. Sauro at the end of the Ponte alla Carraia. Dozens of other pastries are also made here, but the best are these buttery croissants that come out of the oven all morning long.

The croissants are available plain or filled with chocolate or vanilla custard (called *crema*) or with marmalade. If they are temporarily out when you arrive, be patient—there is undoubtedly another batch baking in the back ovens. To consume your treat, order a cappuccino and stand with the crowd around the bar, or sit at one of the stools placed at the counter along one wall.

À LA CARTE
L 2,500, cappuccino and *cornetti*
MENÙ TURISTICO
None
ENGLISH
Some
COVER & SERVICE CHARGES
None

Trattoria Casalinga
via dei Michelozzi, 9r

If you are a collector, or just an admirer of fine furniture and antiques, be sure to walk down via Maggio and look at the many beautiful shops and boutiques selling one-of-a-kind items with prices to match. Try to time your visit to include a meal at this typical Florentine trattoria, which is extremely popular with everyone from students, families, and toothless pensioners to Japanese tourists and ladies-who-lunch.

The two rooms with knotty pine wainscotting and high arched ceilings have closely spaced white-linen-covered tables. Young Levi-clad waitresses wearing high-top tennis shoes and low-cut T-shirts serve the lunch and dinner crowd in a bright and friendly manner. The basic menu of pastas, grills, roasts, and vegetables remains the same throughout the year. Daily specials are handwritten in, and these are the dishes to pay attention to. Because the tables are turned at least twice during each meal, service is fast, so you can count on being in and out in an hour or so, and that is something in Italy.

AREA
piazza Santo Spirito
TELEPHONE
21.86.24
OPEN
Mon–Sat lunch and dinner
CLOSED
Sun; Aug 15-31
HOURS
Lunch noon–2:30 P.M., dinner 7–9:30 P.M.
RESERVATIONS
Advised for 4 or more
CREDIT CARDS
Not accepted
À LA CARTE
L 20,000, beverage not included
MENÙ TURISTICO
None
ENGLISH
Yes
COVER & SERVICE CHARGES
L 1,500 cover, L 1,000 service

Trattoria del Carmine
piazza del Carmine, 18r

Tucked away from the tourist glare is the appealing Trattoria del Carmine, a simple choice where everything always seems to turn out wonderfully. I like to go for lunch or dinner in the summertime and sit under an umbrella on the outside sidewalk terrace. During the cooler months, seating is on ladderback chairs in two whitewashed rooms filled with attractive watercolors and leafy green plants.

AREA
piazza del Carmine, near piazza Santo Spirito
TELEPHONE
21.86.01
OPEN
May–Aug lunch and dinner daily, Sept–Apr lunch and dinner Mon–Sat

CLOSED
Sun Sept–Apr; 15 days in Aug (varies)

HOURS
Lunch noon–2:30 P.M., dinner 7–10:30 P.M.

RESERVATIONS
Suggested, especially for terrace in summer

CREDIT CARDS
AMEX, DC, MC, V

À LA CARTE
L 32,000, beverage not included

MENÙ TURISTICO
L 16,000, beverage included

ENGLISH
Yes

COVER & SERVICE CHARGES
L 2,000, no service charge

The *menù turistico* is definitely the best Cheap Eat going in the entire neighborhood. It gives you a selection of five or six first and second courses, a vegetable or salad, and wine. Dessert, which could be the Florence favorite of *vin santo con biscotti*, hard almond cookies to dip in sweet wine, or *crostata de frutta*, fruit pie, will add only a few well-spent lire to the total bill. On the à la carte side, look for the chef's daily recommendations and his specialties, which are always available. I like to start with the *penne della casa*, short pasta tubes in a cream sauce tossed with mushrooms, peas, and tomatoes. Follow this with the *petto di pollo alla Carmine*, a moist chicken breast with a mushroom and black olive cream sauce. The combination of the two sounds a bit heavy, but they are actually quite light and not at all overpowering.

RESTAURANTS NEAR THE PONTE VECCHIO

Buca dell'Orafo
Il Fornaio
Osteria del Cinghiale Bianco

Buca dell'Orafo
volta dei Girolami, 28r

AREA
Ponte Vecchio

TELEPHONE
21.36.19

OPEN
Tues–Sat lunch and dinner

CLOSED
Sun; Mon; Aug

HOURS
Lunch 12:30–2:30 P.M., dinner 7:30–10:30 P.M.

RESERVATIONS
Essential

CREDIT CARDS
None

À LA CARTE
L 30,000, beverage included

MENÙ TURISTICO
None

Hidden under an archway near the Ponte Vecchio is the Buca dell'Orafo, a favorite for years with Florentines and visitors who know and appreciate good value and authentic cuisine. The two owners are on deck every day to run the kitchen and serve the guests. Everyone seems to know each other, particularly at lunch when there is lots of laughing and talking going on between the tables. If you go for lunch or after 9 P.M., you will be likely to share your experience with Italians. If you go earlier, you will hear nothing but English spoken and probably run into your cousin's neighbor from Detroit.

The regulars know to come on the specific days their favorite dishes are served. Friday it is always fresh fish. Thursday, Friday, and Saturday, *ribollita* headlines the openers, and on Saturday, *pasta e fagioli* (pasta in a broth of beans with onions, bacon, and tomatoes sprinkled with grated cheese) is the dish to order. Every day you can count on finding a special, such as *stracotto e fagioli*, braised beef with beans in a sauce with garlic, onions, and sage. Another seasonal favorite to watch for in the early spring is the *tortino di carciofi*, an artichoke omelette that will change your mind about what can be done with an artichoke. The dessert to melt your heart and willpower at the same time is the house special *dolce*, a sponge cake with cream layers, with meringue and almonds on top. It will be one of the best desserts you will indulge in on your entire trip.

ENGLISH
Yes
COVER & SERVICE CHARGES
L 3,000 cover, no service charge

Il Fornaio
Ponte Vecchio location
Address: via Guicciardini, 3r
Telephone: none

piazza Mercato Centrale location
Address: via Sant'Antonio and via Faenza
Telephone: none

For a sandwich on the run or a pastry to go, you cannot beat Il Fornaio, a chain of bakeries with several locations throughout Florence. They open at 8 A.M. selling trays of hot *cornetti* (croissants), *brioche*, and other breakfast treats and temptations. The lunch lines are legion, proving that when you have the right combination of good food at decent prices, everyone will beat a path to your door. All the food is made to go, and the service is frenetic during the crazy lunch scene. If, however, you go about noon, or wait until after 1:30 P.M., when admittedly the selection will be diminished, you will at least be able to place your order without a long wait.

OPEN
Mon–Tues and Thurs–Sat morning and afternoon, Wed morning only
CLOSED
Every day from 2–4:30 P.M.; Sun; Wed afternoon
HOURS
8 A.M.–2 P.M., 4:30–7:30 P.M.
RESERVATIONS
Not accepted
CREDIT CARDS
None
À LA CARTE
L 4,000–5,500, beverage not included
MENÙ TURISTICO
None
ENGLISH
Depends on who waits on you
COVER & SERVICE CHARGES
None

Osteria del Cinghiale Bianco
borgo San Jacopo, 43r

Massimo Masselli along with his wife and son represent a third generation of well-known restaurateurs in Florence. Their popular restaurant, set in a fourteenth-century tower close to the Ponte Vecchio, specializes in wild boar. This delicacy is best made

AREA
Ponte Vecchio
TELEPHONE
21.57.06
OPEN
Thurs–Mon lunch and dinner

CLOSED
Tues; Wed; July 10–31
HOURS
Lunch noon–2:30 P.M.,
dinner 7–10 P.M.
RESERVATIONS
Essential for lunch and dinner
CREDIT CARDS
None
À LA CARTE
L 32,000, beverage not
included
MENÙ TURISTICO
None
ENGLISH
Yes
COVER & SERVICE CHARGES
No cover, no service charge

into sausage, salami, or ham and served as an *anti-pasto*, or stewed with red wine and vegetables and served with polenta as a main course.

Headlining the many Tuscan dishes served are *pappa al pomodoro* (a filling bread soup made with tomatoes, garlic, and olive oil) and *ribollita*, another hearty, long-simmered soup made with beans, vegetables, and bread. This age-old recipe dates back to the times when peasants did not have enough to eat and had to use what few ingredients they could find to make do. Another wonderful dish to try is the *strozzapreti al burro*, boiled spinach pasta dumplings filled with cheese and drizzled with butter. Delicately crafted desserts include a *crema di Mascarpone* served with cookies, and a *tiramisù* made with ricotta cheese that is light and less sweet than the regular version.

Please keep in mind that reservations are essential for both lunch and dinner. If you want to share your dinner experience with more Italians than Americans, reserve your table for 9 P.M.

RESTAURANTS NEAR SANTA CROCE CHURCH

Bar/Trattoria Santa Croce
CarLie's
Da Benvenuto
Fiaschetteria al Panino
Il Barroccio
Vivoli

Bar/Trattoria Santa Croce
borgo Santa Croce, 31r

AREA
piazza Santa Croce
TELEPHONE
24.49.01
OPEN
Mon–Sat
CLOSED
Dinner; Sun; Dec 21–Jan 6
HOURS
Bar 7:30 A.M.–7:30 P.M.,
lunch noon–3 P.M.

One of the best buys in Florence is leather, and the best place to buy it is around the piazza Santa Croce. The famed leather school of Florence, located inside the Santa Croce church on the piazza, sells everything you will ever need or want in leather. You can also spend a few hours shopping along borgo dei Greci, which is just across from the piazza. Here are countless leather shops with widely varying prices and quality levels, so browse carefully before making final decisions.

When you are in this neighborhood and are ready for something to eat, the Bar/Trattoria Santa Croce is a good Cheap Eat stop where the prices are remarkably gentle. Students with a current ID card from a college or university are entitled to a 10 percent savings on anything ordered. The nice thing here is that you can order only a sandwich or bowl of pasta and enjoy it in comfort at a cushioned booth, without being hassled to hurry on. The pastas are all homemade and are, in a word, fantastic. There is *gnocchi* made three ways: with artichokes, mushrooms and sage, and spicy tomato. The ravioli stuffed with goat cheese and dusted with ground nuts is another special to remember. In addition they serve *antipasti*, sweet and savory crepes, sandwiches, omelettes, ice cream, and homemade cakes and pies. All of this is presided over by Rosy, who speaks perfect English and is loaded with good tips about what to see and do in the area.

RESERVATIONS
Not accepted

CREDIT CARDS
None

À LA CARTE
L 8,000, no beverage

MENÙ TURISTICO
None

ENGLISH
Yes

COVER & SERVICE CHARGES
No cover, no service charge

CarLie's
via delle Brache, 12–14r

In 1988, Carmel D'Arlenzo and Elizabeth Nicolosi, two transplanted Americans from the East Coast, opened CarLie's, Italy's first American bakery, which sells some of the best chocolate chip cookies, brownies, muffins, cheesecake, and apple pie you will ever taste on either side of the Atlantic. They also make birthday cakes and pack tins of their goodies if you want to send some or take a supply with you when you leave Florence.

"Come home to CarLie's" says the sign inside, and many Italians and Americans do every day, in a constant stream from early morning until late at night. Since it has been open, it has become the unofficial American headquarters for visitors and expatriates in Florence eager for news from home and looking for helpful tips and friendly advice about survival in Florence. There is a bulletin board with job and apartment vacancies, and both Carmel and Elizabeth are available to lend an ear to those suffering pangs of homesickness. Usually after a cookie and a sympathetic shoulder to lean on, things improve dramatically.

AREA
piazza Santa Croce

TELEPHONE
21.51.37

OPEN
Tues–Sun

CLOSED
Mon; Aug

HOURS
10 A.M.–1:30 P.M., 3:30–8 P.M.

RESERVATIONS
Not accepted

CREDIT CARDS
None

À LA CARTE
L 1,800 per cookie or muffin

MENÙ TURISTICO
None

ENGLISH
Yes

COVER & SERVICE CHARGES
None

Da Benvenuto
via Mosca, 16r, angle via de' Neri, 47r

AREA
Santa Croce

TELEPHONE
21.48.33

OPEN
Thurs–Sat, Mon–Tues

CLOSED
Sun; Wed; Aug

HOURS
Lunch 12:30–3 P.M.,
dinner 7:15–10 P.M.

RESERVATIONS
Recommended

CREDIT CARDS
None

À LA CARTE
L 20,000, beverage not
included

MENÙ TURISTICO
None

ENGLISH
Yes

COVER & SERVICE CHARGES
L 1,500 cover, 12% service

For more than two decades, Gabriella has been greeting the guests, making espresso, serving dessert, and tending the cash register, while her husband, Loriano Pallini, has been busy at work in his kitchen turning out fine Tuscan fare that the natives rave about. Frankly, this is exactly the type of place that once found, people hate to divulge for fear it will change or fill up with loud tourists and never be the same again.

The three-room trattoria is very casual, with benches and tables placed close together, creating a high-decibel noise level, especially at lunch when people stand in the aisle waiting to be seated. When I go, I try to sit at one of the tables along the window in the large room, and avoid the stuffy anteroom next to the kitchen with three little tables squeezed into it. For best results when ordering, stay with something simple, or the daily specials. For the first course, the rich and flavorful minestrone is always good, and so is the rigatoni with eggplant. For the second course, try the goulash or tuna and white beans for something filling and different. The only dessert made here is a pear tart, and it is irresistibly good.

Fiaschetteria al Panino
via de' Neri, 2r

AREA
piazza Santa Croce

TELEPHONE
21.68.87

OPEN
Mon–Sat

CLOSED
Dinner; Sun; Aug

HOURS
Bar 9 A.M.–9 P.M.,
lunch 12:30–2:30 P.M.

RESERVATIONS
Not accepted

CREDIT CARDS
None

Smart Italian Cheap Eaters eat their lunch in a snack bar. Actually, these are more like bars that serve a hot noon meal. One of the best snack bars around the Santa Croce church is the Fiaschetteria al Panino. You won't be able to miss its corner location—just look for the hungry crowd standing outside willing to tough it out for the food rewards waiting inside. During lunch, it is a virtual mob scene, with fast-paced service geared toward high turnover. Everyone is encouraged to eat quickly at the bar, or to sit on a stool at the marble counters by the windows. Dallying over coffee and engaging in long conversations are not part of the acceptable game plan here.

The food is guaranteed to do wonders for your well-being. Following the Italian tradition of preparing a special dish each day, the chef has *pappa al pomodoro* on Monday, and sturdy bean soup every Tuesday. Wednesday is potluck, and on Thursday expect to feast on ravioli stuffed with spinach and ricotta cheese or a rich meat-filled tortellini. Friday it is bean soup again or the special *della casa, ribollita*. In addition there are always hot *crostini*, pastas, salads, and cold meats. For dessert, I urge you to abandon diet worries and splurge on the chocolate mousse torte, a rich pie that chocoholics will dream of for years to come. You can certainly forget the fried doughnut holes, which will weigh like wet laundry in the pit of your stomach for days.

À LA CARTE
L 6,000, beverage not included

MENÙ TURISTICO
None

ENGLISH
Yes

COVER & SERVICE CHARGES
No cover or service charge

Il Barroccio
via Vigna Vecchia, 31r

For Sunday lunch, Il Barroccio is always a full house with a good mix of Italian families, area regulars, and tourists visiting the Santa Croce church. The closely spaced tables are set with white and red linen cloths, nice silver, china, and fresh flowers. The smoke-yellowed walls have appealing Tuscan watercolors crowding almost every inch of space. The service is generally good, but it can be distracted when the tables are crowded and the two waiters are stretched to the limit.

The thorough menu has all the Tuscan standbys, plus a good selection of seasonal daily specials. All the pasta, sauces, and desserts are made here and are free of preservatives or additives. The variety of starters is impressive, with everything from avocado vinaigrette and shrimp cocktail to a plate of dried salami and ham. The pastas are deliciously simple and recommendable. You can actually taste the potatoes in the homemade *gnocchi* with its fresh basil and tomato sauce, and the rice with *funghi porcini* is loaded with those flavorful wild mushrooms. Main courses to rely on include the eggplant Parmesan, veal fixed several ways, and grilled lamb chops. To end, the ice cream

AREA
Santa Croce Church

TELEPHONE
21.15.03

OPEN
Thurs–Tues lunch and dinner

CLOSED
Wed; July

HOURS
Lunch noon–2:30 P.M., dinner 7:15–10:30 P.M.

RESERVATIONS
Sun lunch

CREDIT CARDS
AMEX, MC, V

À LA CARTE
L 25,000, beverage not included

MENÙ TURISTICO
None

ENGLISH
Yes

COVER & SERVICE CHARGES
L 2,500, 12% service charge

with chocolate sauce or any of the homemade cakes will be a fitting finish to a good meal in Florence.

Vivoli
via Isola delle Stinche 7r

AREA
Santa Croce
TELEPHONE
29.23.34
OPEN
Tues–Sun
CLOSED
Mon; 2nd week to end of Aug; Jan
HOURS
8 A.M.–1 A.M.
RESERVATIONS
Not accepted
CREDIT CARDS
None
À LA CARTE
L 2,000 and up
MENÙ TURISTICO
None
ENGLISH
Yes
COVER & SERVICE CHARGES
No cover, no service charge

The creamiest flavors of ice cream and one of the largest selections in the city are dished out at Vivoli, across the street from Florence's only English-language movie house. It is most active in the evening and at night, when young Florentines strut their stuff, and on Sundays when it becomes a family affair. At these times you will be able to witness the Italian phenomenon of the *passeggiata*, the see-and-be-seen-stroll all Italians love.

Baskets of fresh berries, cases of bananas, and crates of oranges go into the thousand-plus quarts of ice cream that are made and consumed here *each day*. For my *gelato* lire, the absolute best flavor, and one of their most popular, is the orange cream, a cloudlike mixture of cream, orange liqueur, and pieces of fresh orange. Other winners are plum, whipped cream chocolate mousse, and eggnog. The ice cream is served only in cups and you pay for the size of the cup, not the number of flavors you want in it—so go ahead and taste several and you will probably be back for more. A word of warning is in order: Avoid the strange rice ice cream, a bland-tasting vanilla with hard pieces of almost raw rice that are impossible to chew.

RESTAURANTS NEAR THE TRAIN STATION

Da Giorgio
Il Contadino
Il Triangolo delle Bermude
La Lampara
Ristorante de' Medici
Trattoria Guelfa

Da Giorgio
via Palazzuolo, 100r

If the line is too long down the street at Il Contadino, walk up to Da Giorgio, another Cheap Eat with a set-price menu in the giveaway category. When I was there, I thought that Da Giorgio had more going for it than Il Contadino, because in spite of the shared tables covered in oilcloth, there were linen napkins, green plants, a few pictures scattered on the walls, and a larger menu selection. There isn't a printed menu; you must depend on the waiter to tell you what is available that day. For starters, there might be green and white fettuccine or tortellini with a piquant tomato sauce. On Thursday, there is always *gnocchi*. Next you have your choice of meat and vegetables, salad, or potatoes. For lighter appetites, they offer a plate of assorted cheeses served with a green salad. All the wine and mineral water you want are included. The only dessert option is a piece of fresh fruit, but it is extra and not worth it.

AREA
Train station and piazza Santa Maria Novella
TELEPHONE
28.32.91, 23.82.247
OPEN
Mon–Sat lunch and dinner
CLOSED
Sun; NAC
HOURS
Lunch noon–2:30 P.M., dinner 6–10 P.M.
RESERVATIONS
Not accepted
CREDIT CARDS
None
À LA CARTE
None
MENÙ TURISTICO
L 13,000, 2 courses, beverage included
ENGLISH
Yes
COVER & SERVICE CHARGES
None

Il Contadino
via Palazzuolo, 71r

You will probably have to join the line at Il Contadino if you want one of the Cheapest Eats in Florence. Interior decor is nonexistent: Not a picture, plant, or flower of any sort graces a room filled with plastic-covered tables and lots of eager eaters sitting with their sleeves rolled up and their ties loosened. The food is unimaginative to say the least, but it is filling, and for a little over $10 you will get two courses with all the wine and mineral water you can

AREA
Train station and piazza Santa Maria Novella
TELEPHONE
23.82.673
OPEN
Mon–Sat lunch and dinner
CLOSED
Sun; two weeks in Aug (varies)
HOURS
Lunch noon–2:30 P.M., dinner 6:30–9:30 P.M.

guzzle. There are usually five or six choices for the first course, including spaghetti with fish sauce and bean soup. Main course—veal, beef, chicken, lamb—will be garnished with large portions of spinach, salad, or potatoes. Extras include coffee and fresh fruit, the only dessert served.

There is a limited à la carte menu, but everyone ignores it in favor of the set-price meal.

Il Triangolo delle Bermude
via Nazionale, 61r

Rose whiskey, peanut, licorice, after-8 mint, Amaretto-strawberry, and trifle are just a few of the unusual *gelati* flavors dished out daily at Il Triangolo delle Bermude. To do as the Florentines do, you will probably want to order a cup (*coppa*) or cone (*cono*). The various sizes and prices of each are prominently displayed, with the smallest scoop starting at L 2,000. You can mix and match several flavors in a single serving.

If you would like to try one first, ask for an *assaggio*, or taste, which you will be given on a tiny plastic spoon. If you don't want a cone or a cup, order the chocolate yo-yo, two cookies with ice cream in the middle—basically, an ice cream sandwich.

La Lampara
via Nazionale, 36r

For a pizza, a bowl of pasta, or a complete meal anytime from noon until 11 P.M., La Lampara on via Nazionale close to the train station is an address to remember.

The interior would have pleased P.T. Barnum, with seating for 240 diners at one time, a long curved bar where every drink imaginable is poured, a beautiful brass espresso machine, and a pretty interior garden. There is a takeout counter up front, or you can walk by the wood-burning pizza ovens and sit in the back where polite waiters serve with style. There will be something for everyone on the five-page menu, which is mercifully translated into English. While prices cannot be said to be dirt cheap, with care you will be able to enjoy a good meal at an acceptable price.

MENÙ TURISTICO
None
ENGLISH
Yes
COVER & SERVICE CHARGES
L 2,500 cover, 12% service charge

Ristorante de' Medici
via del Giglio, 49r

If you concentrate on one of the pastas, wood-fired pizzas, or an order of succulent grilled meat and avoid the tiny, overpriced salads, you will do just fine at this large, rather formal restaurant where waiters wearing black pants and matching bow ties jog from table to table. I think it is a smart place to remember for several reasons. First, it is open from noon until 2 A.M., and you can go in anytime for a full meal or light snack—great if you have children. Secondly, you can stop by in the evening for a drink and some munchies at the piano bar any night after 8 P.M. Another reason for eating here is the huge selection of pastas and pizzas at prices that won't send you and your budget into orbit. The grilled meats are all the finest quality, and the house specialty is *bistecca alla fiorentina*, sold by the gram. Watch out—this can make your bill soar. Fine Chianti wines are featured at affordable prices, and the mineral water, Surgiva, is considered to be the best in Italy; so good in fact, that George Bush had it imported to the White House. Desserts are all in-house, but for something typical, try the *biscotti di Prato con vin santo*, hard almond cookies dipped in sweet wine. This makes a light finish to any meal.

AREA
Train station, piazza Mercato Centrale
TELEPHONE
21.87.78
OPEN
Tues–Sun
CLOSED
Mon; NAC
HOURS
Noon–2 A.M., continuous service
RESERVATIONS
Not necessary
CREDIT CARDS
MC, V
À LA CARTE
L 18,000, beverage not included
MENÙ TURISTICO
None
ENGLISH
Yes
COVER & SERVICE CHARGES
L 2,000 cover, no service charge

Trattoria Guelfa
via Guelfa, 103r

Trattoria Guelfa is the hands-down favorite of the regulars who pack it to the rafters every day for lunch and dinner. Reservations are absolutely essential, but even with them, be prepared to wait up to half an hour for your table. Service can be irritatingly slow, but when you consider that only two waiters, including hardworking Claudio, the owner, are on duty to serve

AREA
Train station
TELEPHONE
21.33.06
OPEN
Thurs–Tues lunch and dinner
CLOSED
Wed; NAC

HOURS
Lunch noon–3 P.M.,
dinner 7–11 P.M.
RESERVATIONS
Essential
CREDIT CARDS
AMEX, MC, V
À LA CARTE
L 30,000, beverage included
MENÙ TURISTICO
L 18,000, 3 courses, beverage
included
COVER & SERVICE CHARGES
L 2,000 cover, 10% service
charge

the congenial crowd, it is really amazing anyone ever gets anything, let alone have it always arrive piping hot.

The key to success here is wonderful back-to-basics food that is prepared in a loving manner worthy of a real Italian kitchen. If you concentrate on the chef's specials, you simply cannot go wrong. Depending on the day and time of year, expect to find fat green and white tortellini stuffed with ham and mushrooms, spaghetti with fresh crab, or *cappellacci*, three big pasta tubes stuffed with cheese and spinach and served in a cream sauce flavored with wild mushrooms. Other specials include a wild hare stew, roast pork, and grilled veal chops served with roasted potatoes flavored with fresh rosemary. All the desserts remind me of home—especially the *panna cotta*, a cold pudding with hot chocolate poured over it, and the smooth, liqueur-scented *tiramisù*.

Note: Also under the same ownership is Antichi Cancelli (see page 33).

RESTAURANTS NEAR THE UFFIZI GALLERY

Caffè Caruso
I' Cchè C'é C'é
Montecatini

Caffè Caruso
via Lambertesca, 14–16r

AREA
Uffizi Gallery
TELEPHONE
28.19.40
OPEN
Mon–Sat
CLOSED
Sun; NAC
HOURS
8 A.M.–midnight, continuous
service
RESERVATIONS
Not accepted
CREDIT CARDS
MC, V

The medieval part of Florence around the Uffizi Gallery was once a poor and unsavory section of the city. Not anymore. Now it is a young and energized area filled with art galleries, interesting shops, and amusing boutiques. Caffè Caruso is in the middle of it all, on via Lambertesca, the street that cuts right through the Uffizi.

The beauty of Caffè Caruso is that you can eat here cafeteria-style from 8 A.M. until midnight, or until the food runs out. Or, if you want to regroup in the late afternoon and have a cool drink or a sweet treat, this is a good place to recharge your energies for the rest of the day. The atmosphere is definitely upscale, with candles on the tables and local artwork on the walls. In addition to the hot and cold self-service counter, you can order sandwiches, omelettes, and desserts. They also offer every mixed drink imaginable, from an apricot sour to a white Russian. Ten international beers are poured, countless types of coffee are served, and many types of wine and champagne are available.

À LA CARTE
L 14,000, 3 self-service courses beverage not included; drinks L 4,000 and up
MENÙ TURISTICO
None
ENGLISH
Enough
COVER & SERVICE CHARGES
No cover or service charge

I' Cchè C'é C'é
via Magalotti, 11r

In Italian the name means "what you find, you find"—and there is always excellent Tuscan fare and service to be found here.

Owner and chef Gino Noci is a native Florentine with long experience in the restaurant business, including time spent in a French restaurant in London. He emphasizes that his establishment is a casual, family-run place where everyone is welcomed in the same friendly way. Long wooden tables are set with white place mats and red napkins. Ringing the room are shelves of wine bottles and assorted paintings of varying degrees of professionalism. Cheap Eaters will want to pay close attention to the *menù turistico,* which includes everything but dessert, wine, or mineral water. When deciding what to order, always ask your waiter what Gino has cooked specially that day, and also take a long look at the grilled fresh fish. Everything is kept relatively simple, using only the best olive oils and other seasonally fresh ingredients. The house wine, poured from large barrels, is drinkable and recommended.

AREA
Uffizi Gallery
TELEPHONE
21.65.89
OPEN
Tues–Sun lunch and dinner
CLOSED
Mon; Aug 17–Sept 10
HOURS
Lunch 12:30–2:30 P.M., dinner 7:30–10:30 P.M.
RESERVATIONS
Advised on weekends
CREDIT CARDS
V
À LA CARTE
L 30,000, beverage not included
MENÙ TURISTICO
L 20,000, 3 courses, beverage not included
ENGLISH
Yes
COVER & SERVICE CHARGES
L 2,000 cover, no service charge

Montecatini
via dei Leoni, 6r

Tuscany's simplest foods tend to be its most successful, and nowhere is that more true than at Montecatini, a picturesque trattoria specializing in the region's native cuisine. If you are a confirmed Cheap Eater in the mood for a rewarding lunch or dinner, then order the *menù turistico.* This meal deal includes

AREA
Uffizi Gallery
TELEPHONE
28.48.63
OPEN
Thurs–Tues lunch and dinner

CLOSED
Wed; Feb

HOURS
Lunch noon–3 P.M.,
dinner 7–10 P.M.

RESERVATIONS
Not necessary

CREDIT CARDS
AMEX, DC, MC, V

À LA CARTE
L 23,000, beverage not
included

MENÙ TURISTICO
L 20,000, 3 courses,
beverage included

ENGLISH
Yes

COVER & SERVICE CHARGES
L 1,500 cover, 10% service

a first and second course, along with the vegetable, dessert, and beverage of your choice. The selections for each course are good. For instance, you can choose a flavorful vegetable soup; tomato-rich lasagna; pasta dressed with pesto, meat, or tomato sauce; or tortellini. For the main course, there is roast chicken, *trippa alla fiorentina* (tripe stewed in a meat sauce with tomatoes and much, much better than you think it will be), sausage with garlic beans, or fried sole. With a choice of vegetable or salad and a piece of fruit for dessert, it will be impossible to feel any hunger pangs in the near future. Those wanting something less substantial can always order à la carte, but remember that you will have the added expense of the cover and service charges on your final tab.

ROME

When thou art in Rome, do as they do at Rome.
—Cervantes, *Don Quixote*

In the eternal city of Rome, antiquity and history are taken for granted as part of normal life. A leisurely stroll or a bus ride can take you past some of Western civilization's greatest monuments, piazzas, and landmarks. This city, teeming with humanity and choked with traffic, happily lives on amid the testimonies of her past. Among all the cities in Italy—or the rest of Europe for that matter—competing for the title of Worst Traffic Mess Since the Dawn of Time, Rome is the top contender. For air, noise, and nerve pollution, few can touch it. Traffic jams are disasters in which progress is measured in centimeters, and traffic lanes are considered mere suggestions for motorists in cars and on speeding motorbikes.

Romans are famous for *la dolce vita* and for their passion for eating. The delicious Roman cuisine is genuine and appetizing, rich in flavors and aromas. Rome offers literally thousands of dining choices. From the elegant citadels of fine cuisine to the little family-owned and -run trattorias throughout the city, you will eat well here. As in every major world capital, fast food has invaded Rome, but the good news is that serious chefs are bringing back regional standbys and the basic *cucina* everyone wishes Mamma still had the time for and the desire to prepare.

Romans were the originators of the first developed cuisine in the Western world. The beginnings of Roman gastronomic treasures started with the poor, who ate lentils and chick-peas for lack of anything better. Today you will find the remnants of this dish—*pasta e fagioli*—in countless trattorias in Rome. There is nothing fancy about Roman food; in fact, some may think it almost primitive because many of the most famous dishes are based on innards and variety meats such as *coda alla vaccinara* (oxtail stew with vegetables), *trippa alla roman* (tripe cooked with meat sauce, mint, and *pecorino* cheese), and *cervella fritta* (fried brains). The Jewish community in Rome favors deep frying and has raised this cooking method to a delicate art form. Consider *carciofi alla giudia* (artichokes flattened and fried until brown and crisp), and zucchini blossoms stuffed with ricotta cheese and quickly fried.

Roman restaurants are noted for serving the same specialties on the same days of the week. Tuesday or Friday look for fresh fish. On Thursday it is *gnocchi*, on Saturday tripe, and for the traditional Sunday lunch, plan on rich lasagna. Favored starters and pastas are *stracciatella* (chicken broth with egg and cheese), *penne all'amatriciana* (pasta with tomatoes, onions, bacon, and hot pepper), *spaghetti alla carbonara* (pasta with bacon, onion, eggs, cheese, and wine), and *pinzimonio* (olive oil spiked with salt and pepper) with raw vegetables. Popular entrées are *saltimbocca* (which means "hop into the mouth," thin slices of prosciutto and veal sautéed in butter and wine), *abbacchio* (baby lamb roasted over an open fire), *abbacchio scottadito* (tiny grilled lamb chops), and *baccalà* (dried salt cod dipped in butter and fried in olive oil).

RESTAURANTS IN ROME

Abruzzese	75
Albino il Sardo	83
Alemagna	72
Al Fagianetto	76
Al Fontanone	84
Al Pompiere	62
Antico Bottaro	69
Arancio d'Oro	93
Baffetto	66
Bella Roma	87
Beltramme Fiaschetteria	93
Birreria Peroni	73
Bottigliera Reali	76
Bucatino	74
Centro Macrobioto Italiano	94
Da Franco ar Vicoletto	77
Da Giovanni Osteria e Cucina	84
Del Giglio	77
Der Pallaro	64
Enoteca Cavour 313	60
Fiaschetteria Marini	78
Gemma e Maurizio	78
Gino e Pietro	67
Gioia Mia	99
Giolitti	63
Giovanni Fassi, Palazzo del Freddo	79
Girarrosto Toscano	89
Gran Caffè la Strega	80
Hostaria de Paolo e Liliana	80
Hostaria dei Bastioni	90
Hostaria Giulio	64
Il Re del Tramezzino	81

Il Secchio	81
Insalata Ricca	65
Insalata Ricca 2	67
I Numeri	95
La Bottega del Vino	63
La Buca di Ripetta	70
La Gensola	85
L'Archetto	73
Marcello Osteria	99
Margutta Vegetariano	95
Mario	96
Mario's	85
Orso '80	67
Ostariada Nerone	60
Osteria Ar Galletto	65
Osteria da Luciano	82
Osteria St. Ana	70
Palladini	68
Paneformaggio	71
Pasticceria d'Angelo	96
Piccolo Arancio	88
Pizzeria Ivo	86
Pizzeria la Capricciosa	97
Pizzeria la Montecarlo	69
Pizzeria l'Economica	82
Pizzeria Panattoni	87
Re degli Amici	97
Santoro	71
Settimio all'Arancio	98
Taverna dei Quaranta	61
Tavola d'Oro	90
Trattoria Dino	91
Trattoria l'Albanese	61
Trattoria Memmo	91
Trattoria Rondinella	92

RESTAURANTS NEAR THE COLISEUM AND FORUM

Enoteca Cavour 313

Ostariada Nerone

Taverna dei Quaranta

Trattoria l'Albanese

Enoteca Cavour 313
via Cavour, 313

AREA
Coliseum
TELEPHONE
67.85.496
OPEN
Mon–Sat lunch and dinner
CLOSED
Sun; Aug
HOURS
Lunch 12:30–2:30 P.M., dinner 8–12:30 P.M. (open 1 hour before lunch and dinner to sell wine only)
RESERVATIONS
Advised for dinner
CREDIT CARDS
None
À LA CARTE
L 6,000–12,000, beverage not included
MENÙ TURISTICO
None
ENGLISH
Yes
COVER & SERVICE CHARGES
L 1,500 cover, no service charge

For a light lunch or dinner accompanied with a few glasses of fine wine, it will be hard to beat the Enoteca Cavour 313, one of the best wine bars in Rome, featuring over six hundred different wines and champagnes from every wine-growing region in Italy. The casual atmosphere, with wooden tables and booths, draws everyone from workers in dusty shoes on their way home from the job site to socialites dressed to the nines. Angelo, one of the owners, speaks good English and is very knowledgeable about his wines. He will be happy to make suggestions or to discuss whatever wines he is featuring at the time you visit. Lingering is always encouraged, and you can feel free to order as much or as little as you please to eat. There is no pizza, no pasta, and no full meals are served—just beautiful salads, smoked salmon and trout, eleven types of cheese, sixteen kinds of salami, twelve varieties of ham, fourteen homemade pâtés, and more than ten wicked desserts to tempt your palate.

Ostariada Nerone
via delle Terme di Tito, 96

AREA
Coliseum
TELEPHONE
47.45.207
OPEN
Mon–Sat lunch and dinner
CLOSED
Sun; Aug
HOURS
Lunch 12:30–3 P.M., dinner 7–11 P.M.

This classic restaurant is a smart choice for a leisurely lunch between sightseeing rounds near the Coliseum. The emphasis here is firmly on good old-fashioned value, and that is evidenced by the many regulars who have been eating here for decades. The decor is mighty basic: whitewashed walls with a picture or two, white linens on the tables, uniformed waiters who came with the building, hard chairs, and a pay telephone by the front door.

When you go in, take a good look at the beautiful *antipasti* display and the lovely desserts and plan the rest of your meal accordingly. For the first course, hope that the homemade ravioli stuffed with ricotta and sage in a butter sauce is on the menu. On Thursday, you can depend on the *gnocchi*, and every day there is their specialty, *fettuccine alla Nerone*, a rich dish with peas, mushrooms, eggs, and roast chicken. The fish is mostly frozen, so you can forget that. For your main course, order the roast lamb, or if you are in a more daring culinary mood, try the calves' brains sautéed with mushrooms and butter. The melt-in-your-mouth desserts are worth every sugar-charged calorie. Remember, you can walk back to your hotel, or spend the afternoon strolling along the Forum and Coliseum to ease the pangs of guilt.

RESERVATIONS
Advised

CREDIT CARDS
None

À LA CARTE
L 30,000, beverage not included

MENÙ TURISTICO
None

ENGLISH
Enough to get by

COVER & SERVICE CHARGES
L 2,500 cover, service 10%

Taverna dei Quaranta
via Claudia, 24

Even though the Taverna dei Quaranta hasn't a number-one boss, this youthfully owned and operated co-op sails smoothly along with helpful service and unusually good food. In addition, its location near the Coliseum and Forum make it all the more appealing.

The inside has the standard white-linen-covered tables set against a backdrop of stained-glass windows, terra-cotta floors, and wines displayed on shelves positioned around the room. All the ritual dishes of a Roman kitchen are on the menu, from a spinach torte covered with béchamel and Parmesan cheese sauce, to daily pastas, *gnocchi* on Thursdays, grilled meats, excellent seasonal vegetables, and an almost illegally rich chocolate cake. With careful planning, the final bill should be appealingly reasonable.

AREA
Coliseum, Forum

TELEPHONE
70.00.550

OPEN
Oct–May, lunch and dinner Mon–Sat; June–Sept, lunch and dinner daily

CLOSED
Sun Oct–May; NAC

HOURS
Lunch noon–3 P.M., dinner 8–11 P.M.

RESERVATIONS
Suggested

CREDIT CARDS
AMEX, MC, V

À LA CARTE
L 30,000, beverage not included

MENÙ TURISTICO
None

ENGLISH
Yes

COVER & SERVICE CHARGES
L 2,500, no service charge

Trattoria l'Albanese
via dei Serpenti, 148

Although there is nothing overly glamorous about the Trattoria l'Albanese, it is a clean and hospitable family-run choice near the Coliseum. There is a gar-

AREA
Coliseum

TELEPHONE
47.40.777

OPEN
Wed–Mon lunch and dinner
CLOSED
Tues; July 15–Aug 15
HOURS
Lunch noon–3 P.M.,
dinner 7-11 P.M.
RESERVATIONS
Not necessary
CREDIT CARDS
MC, V
À LA CARTE
L 27,000, beverage not
included
MENÙ TURISTICO
L 22,000, 3 courses, beverage
not included
ENGLISH
Some
COVER & SERVICE CHARGES
L 1,500 cover, 12% service
charge

den dining area in back and a plain front room that fill quickly with committed followers who indulge in the rich food that is much more familiar to a working farmer than anyone in the health-conscious 1990s. Dieters need not apply for their pasta specials, especially the *bombolotti* (an egg-rich pasta with sausage, mushrooms, and peas in a Parmesan cheese sauce), or the *cannelloni* (fat pasta tubes stuffed full of ground meat, cheese, and vegetables and covered with a thick tomato sauce). The *menù turistico* is a Cheap Eat joy that includes several choices of soup or pasta, a meat main course, vegetables, and fresh fruit for dessert. Service and drinks are extra, and so is a slice of the decadent Dominican chocolate cake. The low-cost pizzas and *crostini* served in the evening make this even more of a Cheap Eat destination worth serious consideration.

RESTAURANTS IN THE JEWISH QUARTER
Al Pompiere
La Bottega del Vino

Al Pompiere
via S. Maria del Calderari, 38; off via Arenula

AREA
Jewish Quarter
TELEPHONE
68.68.377, 65.43.142
OPEN
Mon–Sat lunch and dinner
CLOSED
Sun; July 20–Aug 31
HOURS
Lunch 12:30–3 P.M.,
dinner 7:30 P.M.–12:30 A.M.
RESERVATIONS
Suggested
CREDIT CARDS
None
À LA CARTE
L 28,000, beverage not
included
MENÙ TURISTICO
None
ENGLISH
Yes

The Jewish ghetto in Rome is a fascinating maze of tiny piazzas, cobblestoned streets, shops selling unusual items, restaurants, and ancient ruins. In the heart of this you will find Al Pompiere, a charming restaurant on the second floor of the 1600 Cenci Bolognetti palace. The three simple dining rooms have dark ceiling frescoes, rustic wooden tables and chairs, and not much else. The emphasis here is on real food for real people at realistic prices.

This is the place to indulge in Roman Jewish cooking at its best. For the *antipasti* course, *do not miss* the *carciofo alla giudia*, a fried flattened artichoke that looks like a pressed flower. Another must, whenever they are in season, are the *fior di zucca ripieni*, lightly fried stuffed zucchini blossoms. Other house specialties include daily homemade pastas, succulent roast baby lamb, *baccalà*—salted dried cod—and *fritto vegetale,* a sensational plate of crisply fried vegetables. The desserts not to pass up are the fattening *tiramisù* and the fresh pear smothered in hot chocolate sauce.

La Bottega del Vino
via Santa Maria del Pianto, 9A

Rising prices for food and services have forced many small restaurants and trattorias out of business in Italy. Coming along in their place are many *enoteche,* or wine bars, that sell wine by the case, bottle, and glass. In addition, many offer lunch and light snacks at very affordable prices.

Whenever I am near the Jewish Quarter in Rome, I head for La Bottega del Vino, where I can always have a nice lunch and a glass of wine without emptying my wallet. Here you will always find artistically arranged cold plates, interesting salads, and at least two or three hot dishes of the day. Seating is in a small room in the back or, better, at one of the tables scattered throughout the wine displays in front.

RESTAURANTS NEAR THE PANTHEON
Giolitti

Giolitti
via Uffici del Vicario, 40

When ice cream is mentioned in Rome, the hands-down favorite is Giolitti, an always-crowded Art Nouveau *gelateria* near the Pantheon where generations of the same family have been dishing out scoops since 1900. In the early morning, fifteen flavors of ice cream are available, along with *cappuccini* and a counter full of waist-expanding pastries. On Tuesday through Saturday, light lunches of salads, omelettes, and a few hot dishes are served in addition to snacks and more pastries. By 2:30 in the afternoon, the lunch counter has been turned over exclusively to ice cream, with more than fifty-seven revolving varieties of pure *gelato* sold to an SRO crowd that appreciates not only the many fabulous flavors, but the premier people-watching opportunities this place always affords.

COVER & SERVICE CHARGES
L 3,000 cover, service included

AREA
Jewish Quarter
TELEPHONE
68.65.970
OPEN
Tues–Fri lunch
CLOSED
Sat, Sun, Mon; Aug
HOURS
Lunch 1–3 P.M.
RESERVATIONS
Not accepted
CREDIT CARDS
None
À LA CARTE
L 4,000–8,000, beverage not included
MENÙ TURISTICO
None
ENGLISH
Yes
COVER & SERVICE CHARGES
No service or cover charge

AREA
Pantheon
TELEPHONE
67.94.206, 67.80.410
OPEN
Tues–Sun
CLOSED
Mon; Sun lunch not served, but gelateria open; NAC
HOURS
7 A.M.–2 A.M., lunch noon–2 P.M. Tues–Sat
RESERVATIONS
Not accepted
CREDIT CARDS
None
À LA CARTE
Ice cream L 4,000, lunch L 9,000
MENÙ TURISTICO
None
ENGLISH
Yes
COVER & SERVICE CHARGES
None

RESTAURANTS NEAR PIAZZA FARNESE AND CAMPO DE' FIORI

Der Pallaro
Hostaria Giulio
Insalata Ricca
Osteria Ar Galletto

Der Pallaro
largo der Pallaro, 15

AREA
campo de' Fiori
TELEPHONE
65.41.4888
OPEN
Tues–Sun lunch and dinner
CLOSED
Mon; Aug 10–25
HOURS
Lunch 1–3 P.M.,
dinner 8 P.M.–12:30 A.M.
RESERVATIONS
Not necessary
CREDIT CARDS
None
À LA CARTE
None
MENÙ TURISTICO
L 28,000, 4 courses, beverage included
ENGLISH
Enough
COVER & SERVICE CHARGES
Cover and service included

The Ristorante der Pallaro will not thrill you with a glitzy location or a snappy interior design, but it is a great example of a chef-owner who really cares what is put on your plate, and, after all, that is still the bottom line when it comes to eating out. The cast of characters in the three-room knotty pine *ristorante* usually includes a lively mix of families, spry senior citizens, a yuppie or two, and anyone else on the prowl for a satisfying Cheap Eat in Rome.

There is *no* à la carte menu, only a *menù turistico* so large that even a veteran coal miner after a ten-hour shift would have trouble finishing. You will start with an *antipasto* and then are served the pasta of the day, which might be spaghetti with marinara sauce, ravioli, or a *fettuccine carbonara*. Next comes the main course, perhaps roast beef, a veal cutlet, or meatballs, garnished with beets, broccoli, or eggplant. Finally there is a choice of cheese, fresh fruit, or homemade cake. The meal also includes a basket of bread and a half-liter of house red or white wine or mineral water. Coffee is not available.

Hostaria Giulio
via della Barchetta, 19

AREA
piazza Farnese and campo de' Fiori
TELEPHONE
65.40.466
OPEN
Mon–Sat lunch and dinner
CLOSED
Sun; NAC

Hostaria Giulio is in a wonderful old Roman building that dates back to the early 1400s. The small inside dining room has arched ceilings, a beautifully tiled floor, and stone walls lined with paintings by local artists. The fifteen tables are covered with light yellow linens and bouquets of fresh flowers. During the steaming summertime, be sure to reserve one of the hotly sought-after outdoor tables on the streetside terrace.

Although English is not a common language around here, with minimal effort you should get by without any problem. The menu features a parade of dishes that change with the seasons. Depending on the time of your visit, you will find good renditions of traditional fare, including ravioli filled with spinach and ricotta cheese, a garlicky fettuccine with pesto, and *gnocchi* every Thursday no matter what time of year it is. Veal and fresh fish are always on, too, along with good vegetables and the usual desserts. When all is said and done, you will not have spent much more than L 25,000 to 30,000 per person, including a carafe of the nice house wine.

HOURS
Lunch 12:30–3 P.M., dinner 7 P.M.–12:30 A.M.
RESERVATIONS
Suggested for terrace in summer
CREDIT CARDS
AMEX, MC, V
À LA CARTE
L 25,000–30,000, beverage included
MENÙ TURISTICO
None
ENGLISH
Limited
COVER & SERVICE CHARGES
L 2,500 cover, 15% service charge

Insalata Ricca
largo di Chiavari, 85

You will find an Insalata Ricca near piazza Navona and another near campo de' Fiori. Bustling with families, foreign residents and sightseers, both offer great value and variety aimed at stretching your lire admirably. For Sunday lunch, plan to arrive early, because within ten minutes of opening, there is a crowd standing outside waiting for a seat. Once inside, everyone sits at closely packed tables, delighting in the mammoth helpings of *antipasti*, pastas, and salads. There is always *gnocchi*, linguine with pesto, whole-wheat pasta with tomatoes and fresh basil, and wonderful meals-in-themselves salads such as tuna, mushroom, or mixed green loaded with raw vegetables. Desserts are afterthoughts on the part of the chef, so save the calories for a *gelato* later on.

AREA
campo de' Fiori
TELEPHONE
65.43.656
OPEN
Thurs–Tues lunch and dinner
CLOSED
Wed; July 15–Aug 15 (varies)
HOURS
Lunch 12:30–3 P.M., dinner 7–11 P.M.
RESERVATIONS
Not accepted
CREDIT CARDS
MC, V
À LA CARTE
L 15,000, beverage included
MENÙ TURISTICO
None
ENGLISH
Yes
COVER & SERVICE CHARGES
No cover or service charge

Osteria Ar Galletto
vicolo del Gallo, 1, piazza Farnese, 102

Osteria Ar Galletto is a perennial favorite because it is a friendly place where everyone helps out, from Mamma in the kitchen to Papà and the boys out front. The inside dining room oozes charm with its wood-beamed ceiling festooned with hanging hams,

AREA
piazza Farnese
TELEPHONE
68.61.714

OPEN
Mon–Sat lunch and dinner
CLOSED
Sun; Dec 22–Jan 10
HOURS
Lunch 12:30–3 P.M.,
dinner 7:30–11:30 P.M.
RESERVATIONS
Evenings only
CREDIT CARDS
Not accepted
À LA CARTE
L 38,000, beverage not
included
MENÙ TURISTICO
None
ENGLISH
Yes
COVER & SERVICE CHARGES
L 2,500 cover, 15% service

hunting murals along the walls, and bright orange linen on the well-spaced tables. On fine evenings, reserve a table outside on the Piazza Farnese, a beautiful Baroque square with fountains at either end. It is an ideal place to lose touch with everything but what is on your plate and who is across the table. A full meal can creep into the Big Splurge category if you are not watchful, but with a little care, and a liter of the house wine, you should be fine. I always like to start with a plate of the hand-cut *prosciutto crudo* and follow with a robust homemade fettuccine dressed either with artichokes or a radicchio salsa. Meat eaters lean toward the *saltimbocca alla romana*, thin slices of veal seasoned with fresh sage, covered with ham, and sautéed in butter with a splash of white wine. The best dessert by far is the *fragole con gelato*, fresh strawberries and ice cream.

RESTAURANTS NEAR PIAZZA NAVONA

Baffetto
Gino e Pietro
Insalata Ricca 2
Orso '80
Palladini
Pizzeria la Montecarlo

AREA
piazza Navona
TELEPHONE
68.61.617
OPEN
Mon–Sat dinner only
CLOSED
Lunch; Sun; Aug 5–Sept 5
HOURS
Dinner 6:30 P.M.–1 A.M.
RESERVATIONS
Not accepted
CREDIT CARDS
None
À LA CARTE
L 7,000–12,000, beverage not
included
MENÙ TURISTICO
None
ENGLISH
Yes
COVER & SERVICE CHARGES
L 1,500 cover, no service charge

Baffetto
via del Governo Vecchio, 114

Baffetto is synonymous in Rome with good pizza, and the lines that form at the front door of this matchbook-sized spot attest to this. Open in the evening only, you can expect to share a table in a tiny room dominated by pizza ovens and a small cash desk. The seats are hard, and lingering is discouraged.

The only other things on the menu besides the pizzas are *bruschette*, the traditional preparation of grilled bread covered with garlic, basil, and ripe red tomatoes, or *crostini*, toasted bread with mozzarella cheese and a variety of simple toppings.

Note: The same patron owns the Montecarlo (see page 69).

Gino e Pietro
via del Governo Vecchio and vicolo Savelli, 3

If you did not know about it, you would never stop, because from the outside, this one is nothing. Once inside, however, you will find a true neighborhood restaurant where bargain-conscious regulars congregate for generous portions of good food and friendly rapport. Remember, you are not here for the classy decor, which is limited to a television set tuned to a sporting event and posters of soccer players covering the walls. You are here to eat, and you will do it well if you order the daily specials or listen to the waiter's recommendations. Particularly trustworthy is the *gnocchi verdi al Gorgonzola* (green *gnocchi* with Gorgonzola cheese), the *penne con carciofi* (pasta tubes with artichokes), and the *scamorza al prosciutto*, baked goat cheese with ham. The fish is frozen, so move on to the sautéed brains with mushrooms and butter. Oh, go ahead, try it just once—it is considered a true Roman delicacy. Tamer diners can have roast veal, grilled pork chops, or an omelette. To finish, the homemade *tiramisù* is worth the guilt trip, but the *crema caramella* is not.

AREA
piazza Navona

TELEPHONE
68.61.576

OPEN
Fri–Wed lunch and dinner

CLOSED
Thurs, July 20–Aug 20

HOURS
Lunch noon–3 P.M., dinner 7:30–11 P.M.

RESERVATIONS
Not necessary

CREDIT CARDS
None

À LA CARTE
L 25,000, beverage included

MENÙ TURISTICO
None

ENGLISH
Enough

COVER & SERVICE CHARGES
L 2,000 cover, no service charge

Insalata Ricca 2
piazza Navona location

piazza Pasquino, 72
Telephone: 65.47.881
Open: Tues–Sun lunch and dinner
Closed: Mon; NAC
Hours: Lunch 12:30–3 P.M., dinner 7–11 P.M.

See Insalata Ricca, campo de' Fiori, page 65, for details.

Orso '80
via dell'Orso, 33

All I want for Christmas besides world peace, economic recovery, and a red Jeep is another great meal at Orso '80, a brightly lit, busy trattoria in the heart of Old Rome. The operation has been owned for twelve

AREA
Above piazza Navona

TELEPHONE
68.64.904, 68.61.710

OPEN
Tues–Sun lunch and dinner
CLOSED
Mon; Aug
HOURS
Lunch 12:30–3:30 P.M.,
dinner 7–11 P.M.
RESERVATIONS
Necessary, especially for dinner
CREDIT CARDS
AMEX, DC, MC, V
À LA CARTE
L 45,000–50,000, beverage not
included
MENÙ TURISTICO
None
ENGLISH
Yes
COVER & SERVICE CHARGES
L 4,000 cover, 15% service

years by two brothers and their longtime friend Antonio, the talented chef. Here you will find truly memorable food served with gusto and guaranteed to ignite even the most jaded palates. Because the prices tend to be higher than most, reserve this dining experience for a Big Splurge.

The restaurant is justly famous for its beautiful *antipasti* table, and I will have to agree that it is one of the best I sampled in all of Italy. You name it and it is here—from seasonal vegetables prepared six different ways to dozens of bowls of fish and shellfish. If you are not careful, you could make this your entire meal. The best of the homemade pastas are those with seafood sauces. Especially recommended are the spaghetti with clam and basil sauce or the *pappardelle al salmone*, wide buttery noodles smothered in a creamy fresh salmon sauce. If you can think about a meat course, veal, beef, and chicken are well represented as is an impressive lineup of fresh fish. In the evenings, the wood-fired pizza oven is roaring, turning out a limited, but delicious selection of crisp-crusted pizzas. After a meal such as this one, dessert hardly seems possible, but if they are available, I recommend a bowl of the sweet fresh strawberries as the perfect finish.

Palladini
via del Governo Vecchio, 29

AREA
piazza Navona
TELEPHONE
None
OPEN
Mon–Fri lunch, snacks, and
beverages
CLOSED
Sat afternoon; Sun; Aug
HOURS
Mon–Fri 7 A.M.–2 P.M. and
5–8 P.M., Sat 7 A.M.–2 P.M.;
sandwiches available from noon
until everything is gone
RESERVATIONS
None
À LA CARTE
L 3,000, beverage not included
MENÙ TURISTICO
None
ENGLISH
No
COVER & SERVICE CHARGES
No cover or service charges

There is no sign outside, no seating inside, positively no charm, and definitely no English spoken in this spartan dive, a great place for anyone whose lire are in danger of running out. Only sandwiches are available, made on slabs of home-baked bread covered with the fillings of your choice, by two old men wearing undershirts and faded Levis. Surprisingly enough, these sandwiches are fabulous, especially the *bresaola e rughetta*, with smoked meat and arugula sprinkled with Parmesan cheese and lemon juice. For your meal, you can either join the lunch bunch and eat your sandwich standing by the cases of soft drinks and beer that line the room, or take your creation with you and gorge in private.

Pizzeria la Montecarlo
vicolo Savelli, 11A–12–13

Many pizzas in Italy are designer-inspired, topped with everything from goat cheese, sun-dried tomatoes, and arugula to pineapple chunks with shrimp and fresh crab meat. At Pizzeria la Montecarlo, the chef does not worry about new fads or the latest culinary whim, he merely dishes out basic tomato-based pizzas in three sizes: small, medium, and "oh-my-goodness," at prices that any Cheap Eater can work into the budget. When you are here, concentrate only on the pizzas and forget everything else, with the exception of the sensational, creamy rich *tiramisù* for dessert, and I promise you will go away full and happy.

AREA
piazza Navona
TELEPHONE
68.61.877
OPEN
Tues–Sun lunch and dinner
CLOSED
Mon; NAC
HOURS
Lunch noon–3 P.M.,
dinner 6:30 P.M.–1 A.M.
RESERVATIONS
Not necessary
CREDIT CARDS
None
À LA CARTE
L 6,000–9,000, beverage not included
MENÙ TURISTICO
None
ENGLISH
Menu in English
COVER & SERVICE CHARGES
L 500 cover, no service charge

RESTAURANTS NEAR PIAZZA DEL POPOLO
Antico Bottaro
La Buca di Ripetta
Osteria St. Ana
Paneformaggio
Santoro

Antico Bottaro
passeggiata di Ripetta, 15

Claudio Vannini knows what he is doing with his two upscale vegetarian restaurants in Rome (see Margutta, page 95). At Antico Bottaro, the mood is elegant and sophisticated. The mirrored walls, grand piano, graceful archways, and columns combine with soft pink linen, heavy silver and crystal, and masses of fresh flowers to create a luxurious and romantic setting, with well-trained waiters sliding discreetly by, pampering the stylishly dressed, loyal clientele.

The food definitely keeps pace with the decor and is, in a word, *wonderful.* Using only the freshest ingredients completely free of additives, the imaginative chef has created an unusual array of changing vegetarian dishes that even the most dedicated carnivore will appreciate. Maybe you will start with the *charlotte de pomodoro con crostini all'aglio*—a flaky tomato affair

AREA
piazza del Popolo
TELEPHONE
36.12.281
OPEN
Tues–Sat lunch and dinner
CLOSED
Sun; NAC
HOURS
Lunch 1–3 P.M., dinner 8 P.M.–midnight
RESERVATIONS
Yes
CREDIT CARDS
AMEX, DC, MC, V
À LA CARTE
L 45,000–50,000, beverage not included
MENÙ TURISTICO
None

with garlic—or the *pâté maison* with pistachios and truffles. The ravioli seasoned with cumin and bathed in a light cream sauce is a match made in food heaven. So is the light potato soufflé with a dusting of almonds. For a lavish finish, sample the chocolate *torta*, or the *degustazione dolci*, an assortment of their most popular desserts. Naturally, all of this does not fall into the budget category, but it will be worth every lira.

La Buca di Ripetta
via di Ripetta, 36

AREA
piazza del Popolo
TELEPHONE
32.19.391
OPEN
Tues–Sat lunch and dinner, Sun lunch only
CLOSED
Sun dinner; Mon; Aug
HOURS
Lunch 12:15–3 P.M., dinner 7:30–11 P.M.
RESERVATIONS
Yes
CREDIT CARDS
None
À LA CARTE
30,000–35,000, beverage included
MENÙ TURISTICO
None
ENGLISH
Yes
COVER & SERVICE CHARGES
L 2,500 cover, 12% service

La Buca di Ripetta is always crowded, a sure sign that the food is good and the prices affordable. It has been run by the same family for over thirty-five years and has the kind of warm atmosphere that puts you in a happy mood immediately. The service is comfortable, if slightly less than professional, but you won't care when you taste one of the daily specials such as buttery linguine bathed in a lemon cream sauce, or tender roast lamb served with clouds of mashed potatoes. Regular menu standbys include wonderful veal preparations, good homemade soups, and a short list of rice and pasta dishes. With dessert, a liter of house wine, and the cover, you should expect to have a final tab of around 30,000 lire.

Osteria St. Ana
via della Penna, 68–69

AREA
piazza del Popolo
TELEPHONE
36.10.291
OPEN
Mon–Fri lunch and dinner, Sat dinner only
CLOSED
Sat lunch; Sun; 2 weeks in Aug
HOURS
Lunch 1–3 P.M., dinner 8–10 P.M.
RESERVATIONS
Yes
CREDIT CARDS
AMEX, DC

The Osteria St. Ana has the warm welcoming atmosphere of a big country house, with stone walls, dark wood antiques and beautiful flower arrangements. People always feel good eating here, because everyone is treated the same. Service, however, proceeds at the usual slow pace, best tolerated by Italians who have come to make an afternoon or evening of it, never thinking of leaving early or of having something else to do.

Good opening bets might be the vegetable *antipasti* or one of the special pastas, perhaps ravioli stuffed with spinach and ricotta, curried risotto with

Also at the top of the first column:

ENGLISH
Yes
COVER & SERVICE CHARGES
L 8,000 cover, service included

scampi, or the *tagliatelle* with radicchio. Fresh fish is always available, but be forewarned: It is sold by the gram and can drive your bill into the stratosphere in a hurry. Of course, there is a full range of beef, lamb, and veal dishes as well as seasonal vegetables and mixed salads to garnish the main course. Desserts hold up their end of the meal, especially the *semifreddo* with chocolate sauce.

À LA CARTE
L 65,000 for 2, beverage included
MENÙ TURISTICO
None
ENGLISH
Yes
COVER & SERVICE CHARGES
L 2,500 cover, service included

Paneformaggio
via di Rippeta, 7A–8A

Neat, clean, quick, and cheap for the area, this bread and cheese shop doubles as a retail bakery selling an interesting variety of natural homemade breads, and a gourmet lunch shop for the businessmen and women that populate the nearby offices.

There is an all-day coffee bar that sells ready-made sandwiches filled with ham, cheese, tuna, or salami. Also featured are daily hot specials such as pasta with zucchini, roast chicken, *penne* with mushrooms, and roast beef. If you order a hot dish, you will be seated at one of the paper-covered tables along the side and back of the room. If you order only a sandwich, you can eat it standing at one of the tall tables toward the front and save a few lire in service charges. To have the best selection and beat the noon crowd, try to arrive early.

AREA
piazza del Popolo
TELEPHONE
36.10.271
OPEN
Mon–Sat continuous service bar and bakery, hot food lunch only
CLOSED
Sun; NAC
HOURS
Bar and bakery 7 A.M.–8 P.M., hot lunch noon–3:30 P.M.
RESERVATIONS
Not accepted
CREDIT CARDS
None
À LA CARTE
L 3,500–10,000, beverage included
MENÙ TURISTICO
None
ENGLISH
Yes
COVER & SERVICE CHARGES
No cover, 10% service at tables

Santoro
via dell'Oca, 43

For almost one hundred years, Santoro has been attracting Fellini and Zefferelli types, plus a wide assortment of writers and artists on the way up or down, as well as legions of fashionable couples who arrive wearing shades, no matter what the weather or time of day.

There are two rooms, both plastered with photos of international celebs and film stars. The best place to sit to catch all of the action is at one of the twelve tables in the front room, or on the sidewalk terrace in the summer.

AREA
piazza del Popolo
TELEPHONE
32.24.841
OPEN
June–Sept daily, Oct–May Thurs–Tues
CLOSED
Wed Oct–May; NAC
HOURS
Lunch 12:30–3:30 P.M., dinner 7:30–11 P.M.

The food is well prepared and moderately priced for the area. No dish I had was anything less than fresh, appealing, and tasty. A good selection of pastas includes a nice *rigatoncini alla carbonara* and a filling *pasta e ceci*. For the main course, I like any of the veal dishes and the tender Scottish lamb chops. For the brave, there is tripe, and for the timid broiled chicken with potatoes. Basic pizzas are served for both lunch and dinner, but frankly, this is not the place to order one. There is the usual lineup of desserts, but they seem overpriced, so most Cheap Eaters will probably skip them.

RESTAURANTS NEAR PIAZZA VENEZIA
Alemagna
Birreria Peroni
L'Archetto

Alemagna
via del Corso, 181

No matter what you are in the mood for, chances are you will find it at Alemagna, a self-service restaurant, tearoom, stand-up coffee bar, bakery, sandwich counter, candy and ice cream store on the busy via del Corso halfway between piazza del Popolo and piazza Venezia.

If you are rushed, choose a toasted sandwich or a piece of ready-made pizza to go, or eat your snack standing at one of the sandwich tables in the center of the big room. For a sit-down lunch, the self-service cafeteria line with seating at linen-covered tables and waiters to serve you is another alternative, albeit a little more expensive than the stand-up way to go. For an afternoon tea and pastry break, or an ice cream sundae that looks like Vesuvius about to erupt, sit at one of the outside tables and watch the passing parade.

RESERVATIONS
Suggested
CREDIT CARDS
AMEX
À LA CARTE
L 25,000–30,000, beverage not included
MENÙ TURISTICO
None
ENGLISH
Yes
COVER & SERVICE CHARGES
L 2,500 cover, 12% service

AREA
Between piazza del Popolo and piazza Venezia
TELEPHONE
67.89.135
OPEN
Mon–Sat
CLOSED
Sun; NAC
HOURS
Coffee bar and cold food 7:30 A.M.–10 P.M., lunch noon–3 P.M., dinner 6–9 P.M.
RESERVATIONS
Not necessary
CREDIT CARDS
MC, V
À LA CARTE
L 12,000–18,000, 2 or 3 courses, beverage not included
MENÙ TURISTICO
None
ENGLISH
Yes, and you can see what you are ordering
COVER & SERVICE CHARGES
L 1,500 cover in tearoom only, service included

Birreria Peroni
via San Marcello, 19

There is no spa cuisine at the Birreria Peroni, only hearty, stick-to-your-ribs plates of pasta, beans, beef, pork, and veal that appeal to strong-hearted men who have put in a hard day's work. With the unbeatable combination of enormous portions and reliable prices, all washed down with tall mugs of beer (no wine is served), it is no wonder that this restaurant has such a loyal following. Unless you arrive early, or go late and run the risk of your favorite dish being sold out, you can expect to stand and wait for a table during the mobbed lunch scene. Service is hectic at best, with waiters shouting orders to a harried cashier who rings them up. Things calm down somewhat at night, but you can still expect to be sitting mighty close to your neighbor in one of Rome's oldest and most atmospheric restaurants.

AREA
piazza Venezia
TELEPHONE
67.95.310
OPEN
Mon–Sat lunch and dinner
CLOSED
Sun; Aug
HOURS
Lunch 12:30–2:45 P.M., dinner 7:30–11:30 P.M.
RESERVATIONS
Not accepted
CREDIT CARDS
None
À LA CARTE
L 5,500–15,000, beverage not included
MENÙ TURISTICO
None
ENGLISH
Enough to get by
COVER & SERVICE CHARGES
No cover, 17% service

L'Archetto
via dell'Archetto, 26

An impressive selection of pastas served in copious portions, along with a full complement of pizzas, makes l'Archetto one of the most frequented restaurants by Cheap Eaters in this part of Rome.

By all means, try not to be seated upstairs with its jumble of posters, fringed lampshades, garlic braids and dried peppers hanging from the rafters, and a display of aging postcards sent by customers. There is just too much going on here, with hustling waiters zipping around as if they are in training for the next Olympics. The best tables are downstairs in the basement, a mix of stuccoed walls, low arched ceilings, and the expected roundup of bottles, pictures, and other bric-a-brac.

The *only* things to consider ordering here are the pasta dishes or a pizza. Pasta aficionados will have a delicious time deciding on which one of the thirty-seven dishes to order. There is everything from a simple garlic, olive oil, and parsley rendition to the

AREA
Near piazza Venezia
TELEPHONE
67.89.064
OPEN
Tues–Sun lunch and dinner
CLOSED
Mon; 2 weeks in Aug (varies)
HOURS
Lunch 12:30–3 P.M., dinner 7 P.M.–1 A.M.
RESERVATIONS
Advised for dinner
CREDIT CARDS
AMEX, DC, MC, V
À LA CARTE
L 12,000–20,000, beverage not included
MENÙ TURISTICO
None
ENGLISH
Enough, and the menu is in English
COVER & SERVICE CHARGES
L 2,000 cover, service included

more exotic *checca* with a cold green tomato and mozzarella sauce, or the *re-faruk*, with garlic, oil, shrimp, mushrooms, cream, tomatoes, and parsley. Pizza fanciers have seventeen selections, ranging from a tomato and mozzarella topping to the Vesuvio, with mushrooms, ham, egg, olives, and salami. Primo dessert temptations include homemade *gelato*, lemon pie, and chocolate cake.

RESTAURANTS NEAR TESTACCIO
Bucatino

Bucatino
via Luca della Robbia, 84–86

AREA
Testaccio

TELEPHONE
57.46.886

OPEN
Tues–Sat lunch and dinner

CLOSED
Mon; Aug

HOURS
Lunch noon–3 P.M.,
dinner 7–11 P.M.

RESERVATIONS
Not necessary

CREDIT CARDS
None

À LA CARTE
L 30,000, beverage not included; less for pizza

MENÙ TURISTICO
None

ENGLISH
Yes

COVER & SERVICE CHARGES
L 2,800 cover, no service charge

Bucatino is a popular tavern in the trendy Testaccio section of Rome. There are three rooms: two upstairs and a large one downstairs. I like the big room upstairs because it is central to all the interesting action and not as claustrophobic and stuffy as the one downstairs. Avoid, at all costs, the little closet-sized room to your left as you walk in the front door.

For the most inexpensive meal, order pizza or pasta with a salad and maybe a dessert. Most other dishes will send the check into higher categories. On Friday, the *pasta e ceci*—pasta with garbanzo beans in an onion, garlic, and tomato sauce—is a wonderful dish. The *bucatini alla mariciana*, thick spaghetti in a tomato and bacon sauce, makes a very filling meal at any time. For diners with more flexible budgets, main-course standouts are the *trippa alla romana*, oxtail stew, roast veal with potatoes, and the moist baked chicken. Those eager to collect off-beat cuisine experiences should be satisfied for a *long* time by the *coratella alla Veneta*: lamb's heart, lung, liver, and spleen cooked in olive oil and seasoned with lots of pepper and onion.

RESTAURANTS NEAR THE TRAIN STATION AND SAN LORENZO

Abruzzese
Al Fagianetto
Bottigliera Reali
Da Franco ar Vicoletto
Del Giglio
Fiaschetteria Marini
Gemma e Maurizio
Giovanni Fassi, Palazzo del Freddo
Gran Caffè la Strega
Hostaria de Paolo e Liliana
Il Re del Tramezzino
Il Secchio
Osteria da Luciano
Pizzeria l'Economica

Abruzzese
via Napoli, 3A–4

The generous cooking is more likely to please a hungry gourmand than a finicky gourmet at this two-room trattoria in the shadow of the opera. Red-coated waiters wearing black pants and bow ties serve a contented crew of diners who return again and again for straightforward food prepared with the best ingredients the market has to offer. The best Cheap Eat is certainly the *menù turistico*, which includes everything from soup to service. The choices for each course are varied and include daily specials. The meat dishes are better than the fish, especially the grilled liver and soul-soothing *osso buco*. If you stray from the set-price meal, you will pay more, but you will be able to indulge in the house pasta specialty, rigatoni bohème, a cholesterol festival of cream cheese and sausage covered with a blanket of Parmesan cheese.

Note: On most weekday mornings, a good outdoor market on this street is worth a stroll through just to see what is in season.

AREA
Opera and train station
TELEPHONE
48.85.505
OPEN
Mon–Sat lunch and dinner
CLOSED
Sun; Aug
HOURS
Lunch noon–3:30 P.M., dinner 7–11 P.M.
RESERVATIONS
Not necessary
CREDIT CARDS
MC, V
À LA CARTE
L 28,000, beverage not included
MENÙ TURISTICO
L 22,000, 3 courses, beverage included
ENGLISH
Yes
COVER & SERVICE CHARGES
L 2,500 & over, no service charge

Al Fagianetto
via Filippo Turati, 21

AREA
Train station
TELEPHONE
44.67.306
OPEN
Fri–Wed lunch and dinner
CLOSED
Thurs; Aug
HOURS
Lunch 12:30–3:30 P.M.,
dinner 7–11 P.M.
RESERVATIONS
Advised for groups over 4
CREDIT CARDS
AMEX, DC, MC, V
À LA CARTE
L 25,000, beverage not
included; L 8,000 for pizza,
beverage not included
MENÙ TURISTICO
None
ENGLISH
Yes
COVER & SERVICE CHARGES
L 2,000 cover, 12% service

Many restaurants near train stations tend to be overpriced tourist traps with uninspired chefs and bored waiters. Al Fagianetto, which is definitely several cuts above all the competition, gets my vote for serving some of the best well-priced and satisfying meals in this difficult area.

The comfortable dining room is hospitable and justifiably busy, especially at lunch. For both the first and second courses, there are more than twenty options to tempt you; however, the Italian clientele gravitates toward the *tagliolini al salmone* and the *risotto con funghi porcini*. Popular main courses include the house specialty, *fagiano alla casareccia*—pheasant—and the chicken served in a rich mushroom sauce.

For a light, easy-on-the-wallet dinner, try one of the pizzas and a salad. With the exception of the ice cream, the desserts are all made here, so go ahead and indulge in one of their cream-filled cakes or luscious fruit tarts.

Bottigliera Reali
via Servio Tullio, 8

AREA
Train station
TELEPHONE
48.72.027
OPEN
Mon–Fri lunch and dinner, Sat
lunch only
CLOSED
Sat dinner; Sun; 1 week in Aug
(varies)
HOURS
Lunch noon–3 P.M.,
dinner 7–9 P.M.
RESERVATIONS
Not accepted
CREDIT CARDS
None
À LA CARTE
L 12,000–18,000, beverage not
included
MENÙ TURISTICO
None
ENGLISH
Some
COVER & SERVICE CHARGES
L 1,200 cover, no service charge

Mario Paziani runs his lilliputian restaurant as if he believes you will be coming back, and believe me, you will, just as all his other patrons do on a regular basis.

The atmosphere inside is chummy, with twenty or thirty people closely packed at the tables and the waiter swapping stories and jokes with the customers. The food isn't delicate or approaching gourmet, but there is plenty of it, and the prices must drive the competition crazy.

Daily pastas, hearty soups, and fresh fish and meat dishes headline a menu that brings back the tastes and smells of Mom's kitchen.

Da Franco ar Vicoletto
via dei Falisci, 1A

Restaurant groupies would be happy to wait in the street for a table here if they could only *find* the place. Da Franco is accessible *only* to the determined first-time guest who is armed with a compass and a detailed street map. Since there is no name, follow these directions once you get to the neighborhood: If you enter from largo Falisci, look for the first door on the left, with the numbers 6930 to the top left of the door. If you come by way of via Latini, turn right at the first corner and the restaurant entrance will be on the right side, the first door after the barber shop called Barberie Michele.

Is the long hunt worth the effort? You bet it is, *if* you love fresh fish. Yes, they have a steak and a veal offering, but they are unremarkable. Stay with the fish for every course from appetizer to main and you will be satisfied. You can start by helping yourself to the fish *antipasti*. My vote for the best pasta goes to the fettuccine with shrimp and artichokes, and the seafood risotto. For the second course, order the mixed grilled seafood platter or whatever is touted on the daily-special list. Most of the fish is sold by the 100-gram weight, so watch out, or your bill will climb. Desserts are mundane; there is no need to save room.

AREA
Train station/San Lorenzo

TELEPHONE
49.57.370

OPEN
Tues-Sun lunch and dinner

CLOSED
Mon; Aug 15–31

HOURS
Lunch 12:30–3:30 P.M., dinner 7:30–11:30 P.M.

RESERVATIONS
Suggested for parties of 6 or more

CREDIT CARDS
None

À LA CARTE
L 30,000, beverage not included

MENÙ TURISTICO
None

ENGLISH
Yes

COVER & SERVICE CHARGES
L 1,500 cover, no service charge

Del Giglio
via Torino, 137

While it is probably not worth a safari across Rome, Del Giglio is worthy of serious consideration if you are looking for a decent meal near the train station or close to the opera. At lunchtime, it is busy dishing out the *menù turistico* to local businessmen who know a meal-deal when they see one. In the evening, the tenor changes and you will be sharing your dining experience with other international visitors who appreciate an affordable meal in today's high-priced Rome.

AREA
Train station, opera

TELEPHONE
48.81.606

OPEN
Mon–Sat lunch and dinner

CLOSED
Sun; 2 weeks in Aug (varies)

HOURS
Lunch 12:30–3 P.M., dinner 7:30–10 P.M.

RESERVATIONS
Not necessary

CREDIT CARDS
AMEX, DC, MC, V
À LA CARTE
L 35,000–40,000, beverage not
included
MENÙ TURISTICO
L 25,000, 3 courses, beverage
included
ENGLISH
Yes
COVER & SERVICE CHARGES
L 2,500 cover, 12% service for
à la carte

The inside is attractive, with high ceilings, wrought-iron wall lights, dried flowers on each table, heavy white linens, and formally clad waiters. Not much English is floating around, but the menu is translated, so you will not end up with sautéed brains when you thought you ordered liver. If you stay with the set-price meal, which offers *antipasti*, soups, pastas, meat, vegetables or salad, cheese or dessert, and wine, beer or water, *and* includes the cover and service, you will come away a happy Cheap Eater. If you stray from this, it can get expensive.

Fiaschetteria Marini
via Raffaele Cadorna, 9

AREA
Train station
TELEPHONE
47.45.534
OPEN
Mon–Fri, 12:15–8 P.M. drinks
and light snacks, Mon–Sat
lunch, Fri lunch and dinner
CLOSED
Dinner except Fri; Aug
HOURS
Lunch 12:15–2:45 P.M.,
dinner 7:30–10 P.M.
RESERVATIONS
Not accepted
CREDIT CARDS
None
À LA CARTE
L 15,000, beverage included
MENÙ TURISTICO
None
ENGLISH
Enough
COVER & SERVICE CHARGES
L 1,500 cover, no service charge

Eating at an *enoteca*, or wine bar, is currently on the "in" list of things to do in Rome. The Fiaschetteria Marini serves abundant lunches to a packed house from Monday through Saturday. Only on Friday evenings are they open for dinner. You must always plan to go early, or be prepared to stand with the regulars gossiping at the bar while waiting for a table. The setting is casual, with paper covers on tiny marble-topped tables set both inside amid crates of wine bottles and outside on the sidewalk in summer. Service is polished, but it can be a little chilly. The daily changing choices are limited, but all are absolutely delicious, especially the *pasta e fagioli*—pasta in a broth of beans with onions, bacon, and tomato and sprinkled with grated cheese—or the *involtini di fagiolini*: veal slices stuffed with ham and cheese and sautéed with beans. For dessert, either the ricotta crêpes or apple torte is a top finale.

Gemma e Maurizio
via Marghera, 39

AREA
Train station
TELEPHONE
49.12.30
OPEN
Mon–Sat lunch and dinner

The sign says Gemma e Maurizio, but the name on the check reads Trattoria de Fabio alla Lupa. Sometimes there is just no explaining these things, especially since Gemma is still running the kitchen, even though her husband, Maurizio, died several years ago.

This appealing restaurant consists of a tiny room with Gelsomina, a calico cat, wandering around thirteen wooden tables and hard rush-seated chairs. Over the years it has become home to a savvy crowd of habitués who always ignore the big printed menu and stick with the daily specials or one of Gemma's famous dishes when available. One of the best of these is *fettuccine alla Gemma*, rich egg noodles swimming in a sauce made from sausage, green tomatoes, onions, celery, and carrots. If you want to make it through dessert, have this as your entrée along with an *antipasto* or a salad. Those with growing appetites or no waistline considerations will appreciate the all-inclusive *menù turistico*, which offers a sampling of the daily specials and homemade desserts. A dessert worth every calorie-loaded bite is the *panna cotta al cioccolato*, a custard pudding made with milk, sugar, whipped cream, and chocolate.

CLOSED
Sun; a few days in mid-Aug

HOURS
Lunch noon–3:30 P.M., dinner 7–11 P.M.

RESERVATIONS
Suggested

CREDIT CARDS
None

À LA CARTE
L 30,000, beverage not included

MENÙ TURISTICO
L 22,000, 3 courses, beverage included

ENGLISH
Yes

COVER & SERVICE CHARGES
L 2,000 cover, 12% service for à la carte

Giovanni Fassi, Palazzo del Freddo
via Principe Eugenio, 65-67

It is said that modern-day Romans hold the nation's *gelato* consumption record of more than five gallons per person per year. Judging from the amount I saw consumed at this century-old *gelateria* near the train station, I think that is an extremely low estimate. Giovanni Fassi sells *gelato* in every flavor imaginable and is considered Mecca by many ice cream connoisseurs in Rome.

When you arrive, look over the flavors displayed in the glass cases with signs in English. Decide what size *cono* (cone) or *coppa* (cup) you want, pay the cashier, and take your receipt to a server. You can take your treat to one of the tables scattered around the cavernous room, or eat it on the run. Prices start around L 1,800 and climb according to how elaborate and involved your order gets.

AREA
Train station

TELEPHONE
44.64.740

OPEN
Tues–Sun

CLOSED
Mon; Aug

HOURS
Tues–Fri 6 P.M.–midnight, Sat and Sun 1 P.M.–midnight

RESERVATIONS
Not accepted

CREDIT CARDS
None

À LA CARTE
L 1,800–4,000, beverage not included

MENÙ TURISTICO
None

ENGLISH
Enough to order and pay

COVER & SERVICE CHARGES
None

Gran Caffè la Strega
piazza del Viminale

AREA
Train station, opera

TELEPHONE
48.56.70

OPEN
Mon–Sat lunch and dinner

Closed Sun; NAC

HOURS
6 A.M.–2 A.M., lunch noon–
3 P.M., dinner 7 P.M.–2 A.M.

RESERVATIONS
Not necessary

CREDIT CARDS
AMEX, DC, MC, V

À LA CARTE
L 7,500 cafeteria meal,
L 9,000–11,000 pizza; beverage
not included

MENÙ TURISTICO
None

ENGLISH
Enough

COVER & SERVICE CHARGES
L 1,500 cover, no service charge

Huge, brightly lighted, and packed with animated Italians—that is the Gran Caffè la Strega, a combination cafeteria, restaurant, and pizzeria catering to yuppie office workers at lunch and a laid-back, eclectic crowd in the evening.

Smart lunch munchers skip the ready-made sandwiches and head straight for the self-service counter. They bypass the diet-destroying display of desserts that appears first, and concentrate on one of the twenty daily salads and ten or twelve hot specials that lie ahead. Seating is inside by the pizza ovens, or on a large outdoor lighted terrace shielded from traffic and street noise by a ring of bushes and trees.

If you want to avoid building up your appetite and frustration levels by standing in the long cafeteria line, you can opt for the section where only pizza is served for both lunch and dinner, and sample one of the twenty-two wood-fired varieties that runs the gamut from a simple topping of tomato and cheese to "the works" with a fried egg on top.

In the evening, waiters and pizzas replace the cafeteria line, but, not to worry, the prices are still very fair.

Hostaria de Paolo e Liliana
via dei Sabeli, 6-8

AREA
San Lorenzo, about 10 minutes
from train station by bus

TELEPHONE
49.17.96

OPEN
Mon–Sat lunch and dinner

CLOSED
Sun; Aug

HOURS
Lunch 12:30–3:30 P.M.,
dinner 7:30–11 P.M.

RESERVATIONS
Not accepted

CREDIT CARDS
None

À LA CARTE
L 15,000, beverage not
included

MENÙ TURISTICO
None

Paper tablecloths, juice glasses for the wine, worn tile floors, a slow-moving fan, a bouquet of flowers in a wine pitcher, and a pay phone and coatrack in one corner—you quickly get the idea that a restaurant design team has never been consulted here. In fact, time has been frozen for years in this little San Lorenzo spot, where the robust cook in her beehive hairdo and sensible slippers comes out and serves steaming bowls of pasta to a cast of locals who have every seat filled by 1:00 P.M.

The handwritten, but legible, menu changes every day, but you can always count on he-man portions of homemade pasta, meaty second courses, and basic seasonal vegetables. Desserts do not exist, except for fresh fruit.

Il Re del Tramezzino
via Mecenate 18A

There is no telephone number to call for reservations at this neighborhood bar not far from the train station. Management doesn't stand on ceremony—only on providing good food and lots of it to hungry neighborhood workers and others in search of a big lunch at a decent price. When you go, check the menu written on a board placed in the front window, then take a seat at the bar that wraps around a colorful *antipasti* display or, in summer, sit at one of the sidewalk tables. The typical menu at this lunch-only spot should put you in good spirits, especially when it results in such low-cost, dependable standbys as *gnocchi*, eggplant *alla parmigiana*, and pasta *all'amatriciana* (with diced bacon, olive oil, garlic, tomatoes, hot red peppers, and onion). In addition to the daily hot specials, they feature different salads, cold meat plates, sandwiches, and a homemade dessert to wrap up the meal. Because the prices are so right, it is a popular destination, so time your visit to beat the rush, because they run out of the best dishes early in the game.

Il Secchio
via Daniele Manin, 30

If Il Secchio were in a tonier location away from the train station, the prices would probably be half again as much. As it is, it is a spotlessly clean and reliable family restaurant that combines sound and savory cooking with reasonable tariffs.

At the back of the main room is a beautiful display of fresh fish, daily *antipasti* selections, fresh fruits of the season, and homemade desserts that is guaranteed to encourage everyone's appetite. In the kitchen, Grandmother rules the roost, cooking the food from

ENGLISH
Very limited
COVER & SERVICE CHARGES
L 1,000 cover, no service charge

AREA
Train station
TELEPHONE
None
OPEN
Mon–Sat lunch only
CLOSED
Sun; dinner; Aug
HOURS
Bar 7:30 A.M.–8 P.M. (coffee and bar drinks), lunch 12:30–3 P.M.
RESERVATIONS
Not accepted
CREDIT CARDS
None
À LA CARTE
L 6,000–12,000, beverage not included
MENÙ TURISTICO
None
ENGLISH
Minimal
COVER & SERVICE CHARGES
L 1,000 cover; no service charge
MISCELLANEOUS
Meals served only at lunchtime

AREA
Train station
TELEPHONE
46.29.81
OPEN
Mon–Sat lunch and dinner
CLOSED
Sun; 5 days mid-Aug
HOURS
Lunch 11:30 A.M.–3:30 P.M., dinner 6–11 P.M.
RESERVATIONS
Not necessary

CREDIT CARDS
AMEX, DC, MC, V

À LA CARTE
L 26,000, beverage not included

MENÙ TURISTICO
L 22,000, 3 courses, beverage not included

ENGLISH
Yes

COVER & SERVICE CHARGES
L 1,800 cover, 12% service for à la carte

her native Abruzzo region in central Italy. Her two sons and their wives, plus a waiter, carry on the rest of the show, making sure that all of their guests are well cared for.

All of the pastas are made here. I like to start with the fiery *penne all'arrabbiata*, short, thick pasta with a hot red sauce, or the *fettuccine alla secchio*, with tomatoes, mushrooms, and peas in a light cream sauce. For the main course, the *osso buco* or the roast veal accompanied with a mixed salad or plate of grilled vegetables is very reassuring. To cap it all off, there is always a creamy *tiramisù* or fresh fruit with a scoop of *gelato* on top.

Osteria da Luciano
via Giovanni Amendola, 73–75

AREA
Train station

TELEPHONE
48.81.640

OPEN
Mon–Sat lunch and dinner

CLOSED
Sun; Aug

HOURS
Lunch 12:30–3 P.M., dinner 7:30–10:30 P.M.

RESERVATIONS
Not accepted

CREDIT CARDS
None

À LA CARTE
L 15,000, beverage included

MENÙ TURISTICO
None

ENGLISH
Minimal

COVER & SERVICE CHARGES
L 1,000 cover, 10% service

Yes, the neighborhood is a bit dicey, especially at night when ladies of the evening cruise the street, but for committed budgeteers, this dining thrill is just too cheap and good to ignore. From the outside, it looks run-down at the heels, but have faith—the cramped and steamy inside is homey and friendly, filled with sturdy locals who have known one another for years and are privy to all of each other's secrets. Remember where you are and don't expect smooth, heel-clicking service, fine china, or gourmet food. You can, however, count on a roll-call of Roman favorites served at fire-sale prices. I recommend starting with a bowl of the chunky minestrone soup, followed by one of their hearty veal or chicken dishes. You can order a side of veggies, a slice of homemade cake, and a liter of the house wine and still get away for around L 15,000 tops—an almost unheard-of feat in Rome's high eating sweepstakes.

Pizzeria l'Economica
via Tiburtina, 46

AREA
San Lorenzo, about a 10-minute bus ride east of train station

TELEPHONE
44.56.669

Pizzeria l'Economica is a bare-bones, family-run place with zero decor that serves low-cost pizzas in the San Lorenzo area of Rome, about a ten-minute bus ride east of the train station. They light the giant wood fires in the evenings only, from 6:30 P.M. until 11:00 P.M., and turn out what many think are the best and cheapest pizzas in Rome. The only other options are *crostini*, pieces of toast covered with any combination of ham, anchovies, sardines, mushrooms, tomatoes, and cheese, or an unbeatable *antipasto* for around L 5,000. Desserts are definitely in the ho-hum category, so pass them up for another time, another place.

OPEN
Mon–Sat dinner only
CLOSED
Lunch; Sun; Aug
HOURS
Dinner 6:30–11 P.M.
RESERVATIONS
Not accepted
CREDIT CARDS
None
À LA CARTE
L 7,000–10,000, beverage included
MENÙ TURISTICO
None
ENGLISH
Yes
COVER & SERVICE CHARGES
No cover, 10% service

RESTAURANTS IN TRASTEVERE
Albino il Sardo
Al Fontanone
Da Giovanni Osteria e Cucina
La Gensola
Mario's
Pizzeria Ivo
Pizzeria Panattoni

Albino il Sardo
via della Luce, 44–45 (piazza Mastai)

If you are in the mood to sit and dawdle away a few pleasant hours over a nice meal, Albino il Sardo in Trastevere may be just the place, especially during the warmer months when tables and umbrellas are placed on the outdoor terrace. The inside is bright and cheerfully unpretentious, with large displays of wines and baskets of salami, fresh fruit, and seasonal vegetables displayed in a big picture window at the front entrance. Indulgent portions of the house specialties of ravioli, spaghetti with fresh clams, and wild boar in season are the mainstay favorites. The usual pastas, grilled and roasted meats, fresh fish, pizzas in the evening, marvelous desserts, and pleasant wines round out the traditional menu.

AREA
Trastevere
TELEPHONE
58.00.846, 58.94.365
OPEN
Tues–Sun lunch and dinner
CLOSED
Mon; 1–15 Sept
HOURS
Lunch 12:15–3 P.M., dinner 7 P.M.–midnight
RESERVATIONS
Yes
CREDIT CARDS
AMEX, MC, V
À LA CARTE
L 35,000, beverage not included
MENÙ TURISTICO
None
ENGLISH
Yes
COVER & SERVICE CHARGES
L 3,000 cover, no service charge

Al Fontanone
piazza Trilusa, 46 (Ponte Sisto)

AREA
Trastevere

TELEPHONE
58.17.312

OPEN
Wed–Mon lunch and dinner

CLOSED
Tues; Aug 20–Sept 15; Dec 22–29

HOURS
Lunch 12:15–2:45 P.M., dinner 7–11:15 P.M.

RESERVATIONS
Advised in summer

CREDIT CARDS
AMEX, MC, V

À LA CARTE
L 27,000, beverage not included

MENÙ TURISTICO
None

ENGLISH
Yes

COVER & SERVICE CHARGES
L 2,500 cover, service included

Joseph Pino, or Pino, as everyone calls him, has been greeting guests at his popular restaurant for more than twenty-five years. The dried herbs and flowers hanging from the corners and along the wooden beams, the comfortable ladderback chairs placed around well-spaced yellow-clad tables, and Pino's heartfelt hospitality make this a congenial dining choice in the Trastevere section of Rome.

I like to start the meal with a small sampling from the *antipasti* table and then move on to the specialty of the house, *fettuccine alla Fontanone*, a rich pasta with mushrooms, tuna, garlic, tomato, and fresh parsley. Other favorites include the *abbacchio al forno*, pink-roasted baby lamb, or a strapping *osso buco*, veal shank with mushrooms or peas. In addition to the regular dining menu, wood-fired pizzas, *crostini*, and *bruschette* are available each evening. Fish is also offered, but it is mostly frozen and uninspired. After two or three courses, the idea of dessert may seem almost impossible, but do order the house *tiramisù*, even if you share it or eat only a spoonful.

Da Giovanni Osteria e Cucina
via della Lungara, 41

AREA
Trastevere

TELEPHONE
None

OPEN
Mon–Sat lunch and dinner

CLOSED
Sun; Aug

HOURS
Lunch 12:30–3 P.M., dinner 7:30–10 P.M.

RESERVATIONS
Not accepted

CREDIT CARDS
None

À LA CARTE
L 15,000–20,000, beverage included

Stop! Here it is, that wonderful little restaurant filled with locals everyone wants and nobody can find. The front room has only nine tables and is decorated with coats hanging from wall pegs, a clock, a few wine bottles, and some copper pots with dried pasta sticking out of them. When you go, be prepared to be squeezed next to a young student couple busy falling in love, a handsome man in a power business suit, or a table full of boisterous workers in paint-spotted overalls downing their fourth glass of Chianti. No one is here for nouvelle anything. They all come for the kind of simple, satisfying peasant food their grandmothers and mothers stopped cooking years ago. The handwritten menu is almost impossible to decipher, so to start, almost everyone orders a bowl of homemade egg fettuccine, lightly bathed in olive oil with a sprinkling of fresh herbs. Ambitious portions of roast veal, chicken, fresh fish, and grilled steaks follow, with the usual litany of seasonal vegetables and salads available as extra garnishes. Dessert choices are narrow, so it is best to stay with the fresh fruit or the cake of the day if your sweet tooth insists.

MENÙ TURISTICO
None

ENGLISH
Minimal

COVER & SERVICE CHARGES
L 900 cover, no service charge

La Gensola
piazza della Gensola, 15

Sicilian pastas and fish dishes prepared by two Polish brothers? Right, that is just what you will get at this simple Trastevere trattoria, and believe me, this food packs a punch you won't soon forget.

If it is on the menu, try the *caponata*, a lusty mix of eggplant, sweet peppers, olives, capers, celery, and clams. Another good choice is the *alici marinati*, fresh anchovies and clams marinated in lemon oil with parsley, chili pepper, and garlic. If you are really an anchovy fan, order the *pasta con sarde* (pasta with anchovies), or the *alici alla Beccafico* (fresh anchovies stuffed with garlic and grilled). Veal-lovers will appreciate the *scaloppine alla siciliana*, tender veal rounds lightly sautéed with olive oil, fresh tomatoes, and capers. Skip the ordinary house wine and select one of the reasonably priced bottles of Sicilian wine to best complement your meal. The only dessert you will need to remember is the *cassata alla siciliana*, a layered sponge cake dipped in Marsala wine, spread with ricotta cheese, sprinkled with sugar, chocolate, and candied fruit, and topped with whipped cream.

AREA
Trastevere

TELEPHONE
58.16.312

OPEN
Mon–Fri lunch and dinner, Sat dinner

CLOSED
Sat lunch; Sun; annual closing varies

HOURS
Lunch noon–2:30 P.M., dinner 7:30–11:30 P.M.

RESERVATIONS
Yes

CREDIT CARDS
None

À LA CARTE
L 30,000, beverage not included

MENÙ TURISTICO
None

ENGLISH
Yes

COVER & SERVICE CHARGES
L 2,000 cover, service included

Mario's
via del Moro, 53

For budget dining in Trastevere, Mario's is a place that was discovered long ago by Cheap Eaters of all nationalities. Here you can forget all about imaginative dishes served with exotic sauces in elegant surroundings populated by beautiful people. Mario's is a

AREA
Trastevere

TELEPHONE
58.03.809

OPEN
Mon–Sat lunch and dinner

CLOSED
Sun; Aug
HOURS
Lunch noon–4 P.M.,
dinner 7 P.M.–midnight
RESERVATIONS
Not necessary
CREDIT CARDS
AMEX, MC, V
À LA CARTE
L 22,000–29,000, beverage not
included
MENÙ TURISTICO
L 15,000, 3 courses, beverage
included
ENGLISH
Yes
COVER & SERVICE CHARGES
L 800 cover, no service charge

remarkably plain, family-run restaurant where waitresses wearing slippers serve basic food with prices that have not kept pace with spiralling inflation. For those who have yet to master the finer points of the Italian menu, here it is printed in English. The *menù turistico* is a virtual steal when you consider it includes three courses, wine, coffee, and the cover charge. For not much more, you can select from uncomplicated à la carte dishes such as spaghetti with tomato or butter and cheese sauce, chicory or carrot salad, beefsteak topped with a fried egg, pork sausage with lentils, or roast lamb or veal. The only dessert other than the fresh fruit is a homemade apple cake made by Mario's sister-in-law. Believe me, you do not want to miss sampling a slice of this rich cake that everyone adores.

Pizzeria Ivo
via di San Francisco a Rippa, 157

AREA
Trastevere
TELEPHONE
58.17.082
OPEN
Wed–Mon dinner only
CLOSED
Tues; lunch; Aug
HOURS
Dinner 6 P.M.–1 A.M.
RESERVATIONS
Not accepted
CREDIT CARDS
None
À LA CARTE
L 9,000–14,000, beverage
included
MENÙ TURISTICO
None
ENGLISH
Yes
COVER & SERVICE CHARGES
L 1,000 cover, no service charge

Some think Ivo serves the best pizza in Rome; others go because it is the ultimate Trastevere dining experience. If you are thirty-something and like a lively, chaotic atmosphere with high-speed waiters and a noisy elbow-to-elbow crowd, you will probably love it, and not even mind standing in the long line waiting to get in.

Inside, the walls are papered with photos of Italian soccer teams and the tables are jammed together as closely as possible—great fun if you speak a little Italian and like to eavesdrop. In the summer, tables are placed not only on the street, but between parked cars. As you can imagine, the service level out here is not brilliant.

So, what about the pizza? Well, it is not bad. All the usual wood-fired varieties are here, and they taste good. With a glass of wine or beer and a salad, you will be out the door for about L 11,000. While it won't have been a restful or leisurely meal, you will have sampled a typical Roman "hot" eating spot.

Pizzeria Panattoni
viale Trastevere, 53–59

The place may not look like much, but it is the loudest, most crowded, and, above all, cheapest pizzeria in Trastevere. If you time it right on a weekend night, you will be able to witness the pizza chefs turning out more than one hundred pizzas per hour to a loyal corps of young-at-heart diners who stop by often to fill up on cheap food. As you can guess, service is casual, and the tables are smashed together in the interest of squeezing in as many people as possible. If pizza doesn't appeal, there are several bean dishes that are really good. Try the *fagioli di fiasco*, beans cooked in wine over an open fire, or the white beans with tuna, onions, or cabbage. Here is all the fiber and roughage you will need for a week! The uninspiring *antipasti* should be skipped, and so should the tired desserts.

AREA
Trastevere
TELEPHONE
58.00.919
OPEN
Thurs–Tues dinner only
CLOSED
Wed; Aug 8–28
HOURS
Dinner 6 P.M.–2 A.M.
RESERVATIONS
Not accepted
CREDIT CARDS
None
À LA CARTE
L 10,000, beverage included
MENÙ TURISTICO
None
ENGLISH
Enough
COVER & SERVICE CHARGES
No cover or service

RESTAURANTS NEAR THE TREVI FOUNTAIN
Bella Roma
Piccolo Arancio

Bella Roma
vicolo Scavolino, 72–74

A meal at Bella Roma will be pleasing to the eye, fulfilling for the stomach, and easy on the wallet. This is the newest restaurant owned by the Insalata Ricca group (see pages 65, 67), and it is destined to become just as popular as their other ones. Tucked away on vicolo Scavolino near the Trevi Fountain, the healthy cooking is light yet imaginative, and you can feel free to order as little as you want without incurring the wrath of the waiters and management.

The *paglia e fieno*—green and white noodles with mushrooms, peas, ham, and cream—or the Sardinian *gnocchetti* with tomato cream sauce makes a terrific beginning. An almost guilt-free lunch might be the farmer's salad, bursting with seasonal greens, ripe red tomatoes, black olives, almonds, and a slice of the special house dessert, apple strudel cake. For a nice

AREA
Trevi Fountain
TELEPHONE
67.90.974
OPEN
Mon–Sat lunch and dinner
CLOSED
Sun; NAC
HOURS
Lunch 12:30–3 P.M.,
dinner 7–11 P.M.
RESERVATIONS
Not necessary
CREDIT CARDS
MC, V
À LA CARTE
L 10,000–15,000, beverage not included
MENÙ TURISTICO
None
ENGLISH
Yes

change of pace, try the assortment of typical Italian cheeses. When accompanied with a basket of fresh bread, a glass of wine, and your favorite person sitting across the table—who could ask for anything more?

Piccolo Arancio
vicolo Scanderbeg, 112

AREA
Trevi Fountain
TELEPHONE
67.86.139, 67.80.766
OPEN
Tues–Sun lunch and dinner
CLOSED
Mon; Aug
HOURS
Lunch 12:30–3 P.M.,
dinner 7 P.M.–midnight
RESERVATIONS
Advised for dinner
CREDIT CARDS
AMEX, DC, MC, V
À LA CARTE
L 28,000, beverage not
included
MENÙ TURISTICO
None
ENGLISH
Yes
COVER & SERVICE CHARGES
L 2,500 cover, no service charge

Many restaurants near the Trevi Fountain have given in to the temptation to feed as many tourists as they can by serving barely adequate food at prices as high as the traffic will bear. You will find none of this at Piccolo Arancio, a popular location where local Romans happily mix with the tourists.

From the outside, it looks just like dozens of others: white walls, beamed ceilings, a bouquet or two of fresh flowers, and a posted menu. If you arrive early enough for lunch, you will quickly realize that this is a family-run affair. You might find the grandfather sitting at a table by the bar shelling peas or stuffing zucchini flowers with cheese. Perhaps one of the daughters-in-law will be doing a last-minute flower arrangement, and another will be helping her husband in the kitchen. The family approach carries over to the service, which is warm, yet smoothly professional.

The food is substantial and creative. The *pappardelle al sugo di lepre*—fettuccine with rabbit sauce—and the pasta with zucchini flowers, curry, and cream are my favorite first courses. On Tuesdays and Fridays, the chef performs wonderful things with fresh fish. The delicate sole with a lemon and wine sauce is always a sure bet, and so is the grilled sea bass. For a light, easy dessert, order the vanilla cream with strawberry sauce.

Note: The Cialfi family also owns Settimio all 'Arancio (see page 98) and Arancio d'Oro (see page 93).

COVER & SERVICE CHARGES
L 2,000 cover, 10% service for dinner

RESTAURANTS NEAR THE VATICAN

Girarrosto Toscano
Hostaria dei Bastioni
Tavola d'Oro
Trattoria Dino
Trattoria Memmo
Trattoria Rondinella

Girarrosto Toscano
via Germanico, 56-60

The area around the Vatican has been declared a dining wasteland by many because of the tacky and overpriced tourist traps that hold out for top dollar, while offering bottom quality to their one-time diners. You need not completely despair, however, because there is a bright star on the horizon at Girarrosto Toscano. This is a marvelous find where the tables are packed with boisterous, gesticulating Italian men and women, many of whom look like they have been firmly planted at the same table, discussing the same gossip or political questions, for the last ten years.

This place is so good and so popular that reservations are required at least one day in advance for seating in the large two-room space dominated by a huge exhibition kitchen and open grill. The specialties here are the foods and wines of Tuscany, and I can promise absolutely that you will not be disappointed by this relatively Big Splurge. I think it is best to get started by ordering the hand-cut prosciutto or a light soup to save room for a bracing veal or beef steak grilled over the coals. As a garnish, consider forgoing the usual vegetables and ordering the *fagioli toscani all'olio*, white beans cooked in olive oil with a liberal lacing of garlic. They are oh-so creamy and wonderful—I dream of them right this minute. If you add a small salad, along with dense chocolate mousse or the house dessert—a cream cake with hot chocolate poured over it at the last minute—you will never be sorry, and you will long remember this meal as a special occasion in Rome.

AREA
Vatican

TELEPHONE
31.47.18

OPEN
Tues–Sun lunch and dinner

CLOSED
Mon; second week of Aug to first week of Sept

HOURS
Lunch 12:30–3 P.M., dinner 8 P.M.–midnight

RESERVATIONS
Essential, as far in advance as possible

CREDIT CARDS
DC

À LA CARTE
L 36,000, beverage not included

MENÙ TURISTICO
None

ENGLISH
Yes

COVER & SERVICE CHARGES
L 3,000 cover, no service charge

Hostaria dei Bastioni
via Leone IV, 29

AREA
Vatican

TELEPHONE
31.93.78

OPEN
Mon–Sat lunch and dinner

CLOSED
Sun; July 15–31

HOURS
Lunch noon–3 P.M.,
dinner 7–11:30 P.M.

RESERVATIONS
Advised

CREDIT CARDS
AMEX, MC, V

À LA CARTE
L 30,000, beverage not
included

MENÙ TURISTICO
None

ENGLISH
Yes

COVER & SERVICE CHARGES
Cover and service included

Unfortunately, the area around the Vatican and Vatican museums is loaded with dreadful tourist traps and even worse restaurants, so finding a decent meal at a fair price becomes almost a mission in life. All hope is not lost, however, thanks to the Hostaria dei Bastioni, found through a tiny doorway below street level on the busy via Leone IV. Inside, the knotty pine dining room is dominated by a large television set that is usually turned on, red and white table coverings, and a kitchen to one side. At this hospitable eatery, you will find moderately priced seafood and a host of other familiar Roman dishes being served to an appreciative public made up largely of business people, contented neighborhood regulars, and smart visitors. The *antipasto rustico*—mixed vegetables—or the hand-cut prosciutto with melon is a good opener, and the crepes with hot chocolate sauce is a great closer. In between you can't go wrong with the *fettuccine alla Bastioni*—with cream, bacon, fresh tomato, and a hint of orange—the risotto with shrimp, a grilled veal chop, eggplant parmigiana, or any of the fresh fish offerings.

Tavola d'Oro
via Marianna Dionigi, 37

AREA
Across Tiber from via
Condotti, near piazza Cavour

TELEPHONE
31.23.17

OPEN
Mon–Sat lunch and dinner

CLOSED
Sun; Aug

HOURS
Lunch 12:30–3 P.M.,
dinner 8–10:30 P.M.

RESERVATIONS
Definitely

CREDIT CARDS
None

Tavola d'Oro is a mom-and-pop restaurant on a busy neighborhood shopping street across the Ponte Cavour from via Condotti. Everything is made in house, from the pasta to the *gelato*. If you are lucky enough to have the right seat, you can watch Mamma in the kitchen busily performing magic on all she prepares. The food is Sicilian, and that means hot, spicy, and very, very good. The one drawback of this postage-stamp-size restaurant is the service, which can be downright rude if, for reasons you will never fathom, they take a dislike to you. If you do not speak Italian or at least have a food dictionary with you, you will be at a *big* disadvantage, because no one will make any attempt at English—period.

If you have never had Sicilian *caponata*—eggplant, capers, and black olives in extra-virgin olive oil—so rich it is almost blue—here is your best shot in Rome. The Sicilian sausage with cheese and coriander seeds is another worthy option, and so is the potato-based pasta topped with eggplant and tomato sauce. To get the full effect of your meal, order a bottle of robust Sicilian wine, and, for dessert, save extra room for the hot zabaglione or the *cannoli* filled with cream cheese mixed with whipped cream. No one said this was going to be a meal for weight-watchers!

À LA CARTE
L 25,000, beverage not included

MENÙ TURISTICO
None

ENGLISH
None

COVER & SERVICE CHARGES
L 2,000 cover, 20% service

Trattoria Dino
via Tacito, 80

For lire watchers in search of a budget lunch near the Vatican, Trattoria Dino is a smart choice. I found this family-run jewel, where Mamma cooks and Papà serves, en route to another spot that ultimately did not make the final cut. Once I looked inside the tiny eight-table room and smelled the wonderful aromas floating from the tiny kitchen in back, I knew this was where I would eat my lunch. The whitewashed rough stucco walls are hung with wooden carvings, braids of garlic, dried herbs, old cooking pans, and pretty baskets. Each day a new menu is handwritten on little pieces of scratch paper and placed on the paper-covered tables. The food appeals to those who love to tackle a serious meal, beginning with a filling *pasta e fagioli*, followed by roast chicken with mashed potatoes, vegetable, and salad, all washed down with a glass or two of the house Chianti. If all this is not enough, there is always fresh fruit or *dolci* for dessert, and all for a final tab everyone can appreciate.

AREA
Vatican

TELEPHONE
36.10.305

OPEN
Mon–Sat lunch only

CLOSED
Sun; dinner; Aug

HOURS
Lunch 12:15–4 P.M.

RESERVATIONS
Not necessary

CREDIT CARDS
None

À LA CARTE
L 20,000, 3 courses, beverage included

MENÙ TURISTICO
None

ENGLISH
Enough

COVER & SERVICE CHARGES
None

Trattoria Memmo
piazza Cavour, 14–15

Home-style cooking speaks to all who love to eat, especially at Memmo, located on the busy piazza Cavour, not far from the Vatican. It is a busy neighborhood trattoria you can rely on for basic Italian food and courteous service from timeless waiters in long white aprons.

AREA
Vatican

TELEPHONE
68.75.065

OPEN
Tues–Sun lunch and dinner

CLOSED
Mon; Aug
HOURS
Lunch 12:30–5 P.M.,
dinner 7:30–11:30 P.M.
RESERVATIONS
Not necessary
CREDIT CARDS
DC
À LA CARTE
L 24,000, beverage not
included
MENÙ TURISTICO
None
ENGLISH
Yes
COVER & SERVICE CHARGES
L 2,500 cover, 13% service

The food is much more tempting than the plain white surroundings. The menu boasts an appealing array of seasonal specialties, as well as tried-and-true favorites that keep the locals returning day after day. Everyone knows that on Tuesday and Friday the special will be *pasta alle vongole*: spaghetti with fresh clams. On Wednesday, the chunky minestrone soup is the highlight, and, on Thursday, of course, the most popular dish is fluffy potato *gnocchi*. On Saturday, tripe headlines the menu, and, for the family Sunday lunch, big portions of lasagna and *cannelloni* are dished out to the regulars. There are also delicious daily pastas and meat dishes, and a guilt-laden homemade chocolate cake for dessert.

Trattoria Rondinella
via Vespasiano, 25

AREA
Vatican
TELEPHONE
37.22.073
OPEN
Mon–Sat lunch and dinner
CLOSED
Sun; 1 week in Nov and
1 week in Jan
HOURS
Lunch noon–3 P.M.,
dinner 6–11 P.M.
RESERVATIONS
Advised in summer
CREDIT CARDS
AMEX, MC, V
À LA CARTE
L 25,000–30,000, beverage not
included
MENÙ TURISTICO
Lunch L 10,000–20,000 Nov,
Jan, and Feb, L 16,000–18,000
rest of year; beverage not
included
ENGLISH
Yes
COVER & SERVICE CHARGES
L 3,000 cover, 10% service for
à la carte

When I asked hotel owners in the neighborhood where they send their guests in search of a good Cheap Eat, every one mentioned Trattoria Rondinella, owned and run by Swiss-born Dora Rietmann. Cooking has been her hobby for years, and she finally realized her dream of opening her own restaurant when all of her five children were grown and on their own. In the few years she has been open, she has managed to accomplish the impossible by not skimping on quality or quantity in exchange for low prices. She personally does all the shopping and makes every dessert, following favorite family recipes she has perfected over the years. The menu is on the long side and offers Swiss and Italian specialties. If you call ahead, she will prepare special paellas or fondues for two or twenty. Her recipe for *tagliatelle fantasia* with ham, tomato, mushrooms, and cream has been requested by *Gourmet* magazine. She serves fresh fish on Tuesday and Friday, and her own smoked trout is always on the menu. The dessert to watch for is her carrot strudel, dense with almonds, eggs, and finely ground carrots. In November, January, and February, look for her fixed-price lunches for 10,000 to 20,000 lire, excluding beverage.

RESTAURANTS NEAR VIA CONDOTTI AND THE SPANISH STEPS

Arancio d'Oro
Beltramme Fiaschetteria
Centro Macrobioto Italiano
I Numeri
Margutta Vegetariano
Mario
Pasticceria d'Angelo
Pizzeria la Capricciosa
Re degli Amici
Settimio all'Arancio

Arancio d'Oro
via Monte d'Oro, 17

Located near the daily antiques market on the piazza Borghese, this typical trattoria is a popular lunchtime rendezvous for the many businessmen who have offices nearby. In the evening the mood slows down and it fills quickly with local residents and a stray tourist or two. Arancio d'Oro and its cousins, Settimio all'Arancio (see page 98) and Piccolo Arancio (see page 88) are owned by the same family and are equally well known for their friendly hospitality and good food at realistic prices. The cooking is hearty, tempting you with wonderful homemade pastas in creamy sauces, sizzling platters of grilled meats, and a lemon mousse dessert no one ever thinks of sharing. Pizzas are available in the evenings only.

AREA
via Condotti
TELEPHONE
68.65.026
OPEN
Mon–Sat lunch and dinner
CLOSED
Sun; Aug
HOURS
Lunch 12:30–3 P.M.,
dinner 7:30–11 P.M.
RESERVATIONS
Advised
CREDIT CARDS
MC, V
À LA CARTE
L 25,000, beverage not included
MENÙ TURISTICO
None
ENGLISH
Yes
COVER & SERVICE CHARGES
L 2,500 cover, service included

Beltramme Fiaschetteria
via della Croce, 39

I cannot claim to have discovered this uncut Cheap Eat gem, because it has been a household word for inexpensive dining for over a century. It is located on a fascinating shopping street that has everything from fishmongers, flower stalls, and fancy bakeries, to luxurious lingerie shops and trendy leather boutiques. The mix of diners also figures into the restaurant's success. At lunchtime it is a home-away-from-home for no-nonsense regulars sitting with napkins around their

AREA
Spanish Steps
TELEPHONE
None
OPEN
Mon–Sat lunch and dinner
CLOSED
Sun; Aug
HOURS
Lunch noon–3 P.M.,
dinner 7:45–10:30 P.M.
RESERVATIONS
Not accepted

CREDIT CARDS
None
À LA CARTE
L 29,000, beverage not
included
MENÙ TURISTICO
None
ENGLISH
Some
COVER & SERVICE CHARGES
L 2,000, cover, service charge
up to the customer

necks, downing their food and wine with earnestness. At night, it is mostly filled with couples who live nearby and a few smart visitors who have been given the inside track for affordable food in this very expensive enclave of Rome.

Beltramme Fiaschetteria is definitely not a health-food sanctuary for the calorie-conscious. There are no food puritans sitting at other tables and rolling their eyes in horror as you delve into an outrageously rich fettuccine with veal sauce, rabbit in white wine, or a filling oxtail stew. The basic menu always stays about the same, but watch for the daily handwritten specials, which reflect the best foods of the season.

Centro Macrobioto Italiano
via della Vite, 14 (third floor)

AREA
Spanish Steps
TELEPHONE
79.25.09
OPEN
Mon–Fri 10 A.M.–7:30 P.M.,
continuous service
CLOSED
Sat; Sun; Aug
HOURS
Hot food from noon–3:00 P.M.,
or until gone
RESERVATIONS
Not accepted
CREDIT CARDS
None
À LA CARTE
L 10,000–15,000, beverage
included
MENÙ TURISTICO
None
ENGLISH
Yes
COVER & SERVICE CHARGES
L 1,000 cover, no service charge
MISCELLANEOUS
No smoking allowed on the
premises

Serious vegetarians in Rome all know about the Centro Macrobioto Italiano, the first macrobiotic center in Italy, reached by a long three-flight hike up steep stairs, or via a white-knuckle trip in a creaking elevator. Let me assure you that the trip is worth the effort, because the food is always wholesome, imaginative, and very good. You can eat either here at one of the marble-topped red metal tables, or take your food with you, in which case you will save the cover charge. From appetizers to desserts, there is something for every type of vegetarian on the daily-changing menu. You can have macrobiotic grain casseroles, steamed veggie plates, a variety of salads and interesting breads, yogurt shakes, natural ice creams, fresh fruit and vegetable juices, and organic wine or beer.

Because the center is a private organization, membership is required. Visitors are allowed to eat here by paying a L 2,000 surcharge and showing their passport. To buy something from the adjoining shop, a L 30,000 fee is levied. If you show your copy of *Cheap Eats in Italy*, however, the fee will be cut in half.

I Numeri
via Belsana, 30

Paper cups, napkins, and table covers along with plastic eating utensils keep the overhead to a minimum at I Numeri, an informal choice close to upper-crust shopping in the via Condotti neighborhood. The fast-food Italian style is surprisingly good and always fresh, thanks to the huge daily turnover for both lunch and dinner. Everyone orders the pastas, and, believe me, they are really good. I like the *fusilli* tossed with barely cooked zucchini, or the *tonarrelli al limone*, square homemade noodles in a lemon-cream sauce. Other favorite dishes are the crepes that range from the house special, with Mascarpone cream cheese and chocolate, to the Honeymoon, filled with honey and nuts, and the Cocktail, with fresh mango and papaya. Feeling nostalgic for a taste of home? Then step right up for a hamburger, hot dog, or roast beef with mayo on your choice of bread.

AREA
via Condotti
TELEPHONE
67.94.969
OPEN
Mon-Sat lunch and dinner
CLOSED
Mon; Aug
HOURS
Lunch 12:30–3 P.M.,
dinner 7:30–11 P.M.
RESERVATIONS
Not accepted
CREDIT CARDS
AMEX, DC, MC, V
À LA CARTE
L 12,000–15,000, beverage not
included
MENÙ TURISTICO
None
ENGLISH
No
COVER & SERVICE CHARGES
L 2,000 cover, no service
charge

Margutta Vegetariano
via Margutta, 119

You won't find drab people munching brown rice cakes and thumbing through yoga manuals at Margutta, an upscale vegetarian restaurant owned by Claudio Vannini, who also has Antico Bottaro (see page 69). At Margutta, you can depend on delicious vegetarian food served in a relaxed, open, California-style atmosphere with well-spaced mahogany tables, comfortable cushioned chairs, attractive plants, and helpful waiters. The chef deserves awards for creating inventive dishes for every course. All the pastas are made here. Some of the interesting choices include a ravioli stuffed with ricotta and cumin and covered in a light spinach sauce. *Rigatoni alla carbonara vegetale* is another winner with its light cream sauce drizzled over *al dente* vegetables and rigatoni noodles. The salads are enormous and, if you are not starving, could be meals in themselves when accompanied with whole-grain bread and a fancy dessert. I like the

AREA
Spanish Steps
TELEPHONE
67.86.033
OPEN
Mon–Sun lunch and dinner
CLOSED
Sun; Aug
HOURS
Lunch 1–3 P.M.,
dinner 8–11 P.M.
RESERVATIONS
Necessary for dinner
CREDIT CARDS
AMEX, DC, MC, V
À LA CARTE
L 32,000, beverage not
included
MENÙ TURISTICO
None
ENGLISH
Yes

insalata alla greca, full of tomatoes, cucumbers, peppers, onions, black olives, feta cheese, and yogurt. Alluring main-course plates include a crepe stuffed with fresh artichokes, a nicely grilled vegetable assortment, or a zucchini soufflé with a tart green salsa. Desserts are worth serious cheating on your diet, especially the chocolate cheesecake and the lemon torte. Organic wines and beers are served along with a complement of herbal teas.

Mario
via della Vite, 55

AREA
Spanish Steps
TELEPHONE
67.83.818
OPEN
Mon–Sat lunch and dinner
CLOSED
Sun; Aug
HOURS
Lunch 12:30–3 P.M.,
dinner 7–11 P.M.
RESERVATIONS
Necessary
CREDIT CARDS
AMEX, DC, MC, V
À LA CARTE
L 35,000, beverage not
included
MENÙ TURISTICO
None
ENGLISH
Yes
COVER & SERVICE CHARGES
L 4,000 cover, no service charge

No one ever comes to pick and nibble at Mario's, a typical Tuscan-style trattoria with whitewashed walls, raffia-covered chairs, bottles of Chianti on the tables, and service that ranges from friendly and attentive to distracted and rather slow. It is a popular eating destination for both Romans and visitors, and the crowded atmosphere is part of the total experience of being here. Because of the crunch during prime time, please keep in mind that you must always arrive with a reservation.

This is definitely the place to sample classic Tuscan fare, including *ribollita,* a heavy bread-thickened soup, and the famous *bistecca alla fiorentina,* a big steak rubbed with olive oil and herbs and grilled until just pink. Other dishes to consider are the braised beef with polenta, and the wild boar and pheasant when they are in season. For dessert, I recommend zeroing in on the *tiramisù,* a liqueur-soaked layering of cake, Marsala wine, espresso coffee, and creamy Mascarpone cheese.

Pasticceria d'Angelo
via della Croce, 29–30

AREA
Spanish Steps, via Condotti
TELEPHONE
67.83.924
OPEN
Wed–Mon lunch and dinner
CLOSED
Tues; Aug
HOURS
Bar and pastries 7 A.M.–8 P.M.;
lunch 12:30–3 P.M.

For power snacking or lunching, the Pasticceria d'Angelo in the heart of Rome's premier shopping district is a *must.* It is open from 7 A.M. until 8 P.M., with continuous service from the bar and pastry counter, and lunch service from 12:30 P.M. until 3 P.M. Between shopping sprints, you can order lunch from the see-through cafeteria line, where the daily offerings include assorted *antipasti*, salads, soups, several pastas, and grilled meats.

The nice thing about eating here is that you can have just a bowl of soup or indulge in a four-course blow-out if you are stoking up for heavy-duty afternoon shopping rounds. Freshly made sandwiches are also available, but for these you will have to stand at one of the bar tables in front. If you are on the run, or want something for later, ask to have it wrapped to go: *da portare via.*

RESERVATIONS
Not necessary
CREDIT CARDS
AMEX, DC, MC, V
À LA CARTE
L 8,000–10,000, 2-course lunch; L 3,500 sandwiches; beverage not included
MENÙ TURISTICO
None
ENGLISH
Yes
COVER & SERVICE CHARGES
L 1,500 cover for tables, no service charge

Pizzeria la Capricciosa
largo dei Lombardi, 8

Pizzeria la Capricciosa is a culinary coliseum serving Italians and an international crowd of breezy visitors. While not the place to go for an elegant evening on the town, it is one to consider for a typically basic Italian meal with virtually no surprises. Over 250 meals per day are served by fast-footed waiters to hungry people sitting at tables with little spaces in between. There is bound to be something for everyone on a menu that lists 8 *antipasti*, 19 pastas, over 30 meat and fish possibilities, 16 pizza combinations in the evening, and more desserts than most pastry shops offer.

All of this is yours from Wednesday through Monday, at prices that do not require any major budget sacrifices.

AREA
via Condotti
TELEPHONE
67.94.027
OPEN
Wed–Mon lunch and dinner
CLOSED
Tues; 15 days in Aug (varies)
HOURS
Lunch 12:30–3 P.M., dinner 7 P.M.–1 A.M.
RESERVATIONS
Not necessary
CREDIT CARDS
AMEX, MC, V
À LA CARTE
L 23,000, beverage not included; L 9,000, pizza, beverage not included
MENÙ TURISTICO
None
ENGLISH
Yes
COVER & SERVICE CHARGES
L 2,000 cover, no service charge

Re degli Amici
via della Croce, 33B

The five-room restaurant with red-and-white-cloth-covered tables, murals on the ceilings, local artists' works lining the walls, and brash waiters racing about is a Roman institution. People continue to come here for the classic cooking style characteristic of a trattoria that serves multiple-choice *antipasti*, a long list of pastas, succulent grilled meats, and wood-fired pizzas to hungry audiences both day and night. Re degli Amici also upholds the longstanding Roman

AREA
Spanish Steps, via Condotti
TELEPHONE
67.95.380, 67.82.555
OPEN
Tues–Sun lunch and dinner
CLOSED
Mon; first 2 weeks July
HOURS
Lunch 12:30–3 P.M., dinner 7:30–10 P.M.
RESERVATIONS
Advised for dinner

CREDIT CARDS
AMEX, DC, MC, V
À LA CARTE
L 38,000, beverage not
included; L 15,000 pizza at
dinner, beverage not included
MENÙ TURISTICO
None
ENGLISH
Yes
COVER & SERVICE CHARGES
L 3,000 cover, no service charge

tradition of serving a particular dish on certain days of the week. From Monday through Wednesday, you are on your own, but on Thursday, you can count on *gnocchi*, Friday it is *baccalà* (dried salted cod), the Saturday special is tripe, and on Sundays you will find lasagna. *Warning*: if you want this dining experience to fall into the really Cheap Eat category in the evening, order a pizza and a salad and you will be budget wise and happily contented.

Settimio all'Arancio
via dell'Arancio, 50

AREA
via Condotti
TELEPHONE
68.76.119
OPEN
Mon–Sat lunch and dinner
CLOSED
Sun; Aug
HOURS
Lunch 12:30–3:30 P.M.,
dinner 6–11:30 P.M.
RESERVATIONS
Recommended
CREDIT CARDS
AMEX, DC, MC, V
À LA CARTE
L 25,000, beverage not included
MENÙ TURISTICO
None
ENGLISH
Some
COVER & SERVICE CHARGES
L 3,000 cover per person, no
service charge

Settimio all'Arancio was very close to my apartment in Rome, so I came to know it well. It is one of three excellent restaurants run by the Cialfi family; the other two are Arancio d'Oro (see page 93) and Piccolo Arancio (see page 88). The mood here is exactly right for a neighborhood trattoria, with wholesome, well-prepared food served in a small whitewashed dining room with bright yellow table linens and a few fresh flowers.

The best appetizers to remember are the *fiori di zucchino*, zucchini flowers stuffed with cheese, and the deep-fried artichokes. I also love their *fusilli alla melanzana*—pasta with eggplant—and *penne* with artichokes. On Fridays, I recommend ordering any of their fresh fish dishes, which are cooked to perfection.

Dreamy desserts include chocolate or lemon mousse and a *tiramisù* to behold.

Gioia Mia
via degli Avignonesi, 34

Gioia Mia has a well-deserved reputation for consistently good food, good service, and good prices. When you arrive, the tantalizing smells and rushed waiters serving an elbow-to-elbow crowd tell you this will be good—and it is. The inside is typical trattoria style, with hanging sausages and peppers, bowls of fresh fruit and vegetables in the window, and wines displayed on shelves.

Smart diners often skip the tempting *antipasti* table and begin their feast with one of the twenty-five or thirty pasta offerings. There is something here for everyone, from *gnocchi*, crepes, *cannelloni*, and spaghetti, to risotto and ravioli. In the same hearty vein are dozens of wood-fired pizzas and several *calzone*. Carnivores will be hard-pressed to decide between all the veal offerings, including the kidneys with Cognac or truffles and wild mushrooms, and the beautifully grilled baby lamb chops. Those with trencherman appetites can attack the one-pound *bistecca alla fiorentina*: an enormous grilled steak that is really enough for three people. The desserts to keep in mind, if you can possibly do it, are the *mille foglie della casa*—a flaky pastry layered with thick cream, chocolate, and whipped cream—and the *pera alla Gioia*, a pear and chocolate cake with a cream frosting.

AREA
Near beginning of via Veneto

TELEPHONE
48.82.784

OPEN
Mon–Sat lunch and dinner

CLOSED
Sun; Aug

HOURS
Lunch 12:15–3 P.M., dinner 7:00–11 P.M.

RESERVATIONS
Suggested

CREDIT CARDS
AMEX, DC, MC, V

À LA CARTE
L 30,000, beverage not included

MENÙ TURISTICO
None

ENGLISH
Yes

COVER & SERVICE CHARGES
L 2,500 cover, no service charge

Marcello Osteria
via Aurora, 37

Restaurants in the via Veneto neighborhood are notoriously high-priced, but this is not the case at Marcello, an amicably cramped, two-room dining choice with barely enough seats for fifty-five people. Sports fans will enjoy the collection of old and new posters depicting the Olympics, football, boxing, bullfighting, and soccer World Cup championships. Ev-

AREA
via Veneto

TELEPHONE
48.19.467

OPEN
Mon–Sat lunch and dinner

CLOSED
Sun; NAC

HOURS
Lunch 1–4 P.M.,
dinner 7:30 P.M.–2 A.M.

RESERVATIONS
Advised for both lunch and
dinner

CREDIT CARDS
AMEX, DC, MC, V

À LA CARTE
L 30,000, beverage not
included

MENÙ TURISTICO
None

ENGLISH
Yes

COVER & SERVICE CHARGES
L 2,000 cover, 15% service

eryone will enjoy the simply wonderful food and service that have made this a favorite for years.

The cook knows how to turn out imaginative dishes with superb finesse. The *antipasti* table is a delightfully rich assortment of the freshest foods the market has during the season. The pasta selections are long, and all are good, especially the *gnocchi* on Thursday served with veal roast and piles of fresh vegetables. Another winner is the *pasta mista alla romana*, three different pastas with three sauces. Along with an *antipasto* and a salad, this pasta is a meal in itself. The main courses lean heavily toward veal prepared in different ways. One of the best presentations is the *paillard ripiena*, a veal scallop with asparagus and cheese, baked in red wine. Top off the meal with one of the homemade dessert cakes or a dish of creamy *gelato*, then sit back with a strong espresso and savor the time-honored combination of a generous yet affordable meal.

VENICE

> When I went to Venice, my dream became my address.
> —Marcel Proust, 1906

Founded over fifteen-hundred years ago on a cluster of mud flats, Venice became Europe's trading post between the East and West, reaching the height of its power in the fifteenth century. Although it no longer enjoys the same trading status, it remains a glorious reflection of its rich past, while depending for income largely on the masses of visitors who arrive every year to marvel at her glorious relics.

In Venice, one always has the feeling of being suspended somewhere in time. Little has changed here over the centuries to diminish the harmony of colors, lights, sounds, and smells that float dreamlike over the canals and lagoons. Composed of more than 100 islets and 150 canals linked together by 400 bridges, it is little wonder that getting lost is so easy, even for a native. However, becoming hopelessly lost in the maze of back streets, *rios*, and *campos* will be one of the most pleasurable experiences of your time spent in this romantic city on the Adriatic.

Since you can't drive a car, hop a bus, or hail a cab—at least not on land—what you will do in Venice is walk, walk, and walk. To save yourself supreme confusion, it is necessary to buy a good map and become familiar with the six districts, or *sestieri*, that make up the city. They are San Marco, Castello, Cannaregio, San Polo, Dorsoduro, and Santa Croce. Addresses are usually given by the district and number (Dorsoduro 3456) and very often omit the street. To help you as much as possible, all the listings in the Venice section of *Cheap Eats in Italy* include the name of the street, the number, and the *sestiere* (calle dell'Oca, 3456, Dorsoduro). This will help, but it is not foolproof, because street names may repeat in more than one *sestiere*, some buildings have more than one set of numbers, and addresses close to one another mathematically may be on buildings on opposite ends of the *sestiere*, because within each *sestiere* there are some six thousand numbers with no clear-cut sequence. It is no wonder that hair tearing and frustration in the extreme can result if too much logic is expected.

Though you may be lost, don't panic—just use the yellow signs posted throughout the city to head in the direction you want. For example, look for the sign saying Rialto: the bridge that connects the San Marco district with San Polo. Accademia is your direction if you want to be in Dorsoduro and see the Guggenheim collection. If you are going to Santa Croce, look for signs saying Piazzale Roma, and if you are going to Cannaregio, you will want the *ferrovia* (train station).

Venice celebrates a number of holidays (*feste*). The most important is Carnivale, held during the ten days before Lent and ending on Shrove Tuesday with a masked ball for the elite and dancing in St. Mark's Square for the rest of us. Crowds during this time are legion. Unless you enjoy elbow-to-elbow mob scenes and a "the-sky-is-the-limit" price structure in hotels and restaurants, it is best to avoid this time in Venice.

If you think food is expensive in Florence and Rome, you haven't yet been to Venice, where even for Italians used to runaway inflation, dining out is considered expensive. While Venice is a city of romantic enchantment, the high cost of living here, plus the endless flow of tourists, keeps the prices in the stratosphere. The best word-of-mouth recommendation for a Venetian restaurant is that the prices are not *too* high. My own feeling is that the short-term visitor to Venice should seriously consider casting aside thoughts of great economy and take the philosophical view that he or she may never pass this way again. This is not to say that good-value restaurants do not exist, because they do and I have found many for you. It is just a warning that you will spend more for food in Venice than you want to.

One good way to shave food costs is to lunch at a snack bar. Most Venetians do, and many order a plate of *cicchetti*: little appetizers similar to Spanish tapas. Another option is a plump *tramezzino*: a sandwich filled with almost anything you can think of. The Cheapest Eat will be a picnic you make up yourself from foods bought at the market or deli. Venetian cuisine is based on the sea: *granseole* (spider crabs), *molecche* (soft-shell crabs), *seppie in nero* (squid cooked in its own black ink and usually served with pasta or polenta). Risotto is the favored starch, sauced with delicate seafood or tender greens. Polenta appears not only with fish, but with the famous *fegato alla veneziana*: calves' liver with onions. For dessert, the creamy *tiramisù* (which literally means "pick-me-up") is made with Mascarpone cheese, cream, espresso, ladyfingers, and chocolate and spiked with liqueur or rum.

RESTAURANTS IN VENICE, GIUDECCA, LIDO, AND MURANO
VENICE

Ae Oche	133
Ai Cugnai	113
Ai Gondolieri	114
Ai Promessi Sposi	105
Al Covo	110
Al Gobbo di Rialto	126
Aliani Gastronomia	127

Alla Maddalena   105
Alla Madonna   127
All'Antico Pizzo   128
Al Milion   129
Antica Locanda Montin   115
Antica Trattoria da Nino   106
Antico Capon   116
Bella Venezia   106
Bora Bora   121
Brodo di Giuggiole   134
Ca' d'Oro   107
Caffè dei Frari   129
Cantina do Spade   130
Cip Ciap   111
Crepizza   116
Da Bepi   108
Da Marco   130
Da Nico   121
Do Mori   131
Fiore   122
Friggitoria da Bruno   117
Gelati Nico   117
Ignazio   131
Il Doge Gelaterie   118
Il Melograno   108
La Zucca   134
Leon Bianco   123
L'Incontro   118
Osteria ai Assassini   123
Paolin   124
Premiata Latteria Zorzi   124
Ristorante al Ponte   109
Rosticceria S. Bartolomeo   125
Sempione   125
Taverna San Trovaso   119
Tonolo   120
Trattoria alle Burchielle   135
Trattoria Pizzeria San Tomà   132
Trattoria Rivetta   112
Trattoria Tofanelli   112

GIUDECCA

Altanella   136

LIDO

Favorita   137

Pizzeria da Massimo   138

Ristorante Belvedere e Tavola Calda   138

MURANO

Ai Vetrai   139

Antica Trattoria Muranese   140

RESTAURANTS IN CANNAREGIO

Ai Promessi Sposi
Alla Maddalena
Antica Trattoria da Nino
Bella Venezia
Ca' d'Oro
Da Bepi
Il Melograno
Ristorante al Ponte

Ai Promessi Sposi
calle dell'Oca, 4337

Ai Promessi Sposi is a young and friendly hostaria where portions are abundant and the quality of the food is as unbeatable as the prices, which remain comfortably in the lower ranges. The set-price menu is a budgeteer's dream because it is filling and includes all of the chef's specialties. There is spaghetti *bigoli in salsa* (pasta with anchovies and onions), *sarde in saor* (marinated sardines with anchovies), and *baccalà manteccato* (cod stew). Included with the main course are assorted grilled vegetables or a tasty vegetable stew with peppers and eggplant. If you are not hungry for the three-course bonanza, ask for the pasta and salad special that goes for L 10,000, cover included. A liter of house wine to accompany your meal sells for only L 6,000, a price seldom seen anywhere in Venice these days. If you only want to grab a bite on the go, their stand-up bar offers some of the cheapest and best *cicchetti* (appetizers) in the neighborhood.

AREA
Cannaregio
TELEPHONE
52.28.609
OPEN
Thurs–Tues lunch and dinner
CLOSED
Wed; NAC
HOURS
Bar 8 A.M.–2:30 P.M. and 4:30–10 P.M., lunch noon–2:30 P.M., dinner 7–10 P.M.
RESERVATIONS
Not necessary
CREDIT CARDS
None
À LA CARTE
L 25,000, beverage not included
MENÙ TURISTICO
L 14,000, 3 courses, beverage not included; L 10,000, pasta and salad only
ENGLISH
Yes
COVER & SERVICE CHARGES
L 2,000 cover, 12% service

Alla Maddalena
rio Terra della Maddalena, 2348

Where to go when you find yourself stranded in the dining desert around the train station and do not want to settle for the unappetizing tourist food that is the rule rather than the exception here? One answer is Alla Maddalena, a fine place to come for a sandwich, plate of rigatoni, *tagliatelle*, or the daily special. All the food is made fresh daily and in some cases is in limited supply, so when they run out of roast beef or the pasta

AREA
Cannaregio
TELEPHONE
72.07.23
OPEN
Mon–Sat lunch and sandwiches
CLOSED
Sun; Aug
HOURS
7:30 A.M.–9 P.M.; lunch 12:30–2 P.M.
RESERVATIONS
Not accepted

of the day, you are out of luck. Desserts are brought in, so it is better to go to the *gelateria* across the street and have an ice cream cone. At Alla Maddalena, you can enjoy your repast standing at the bar and kibitzing with the friendly barmen, or sitting on a tall stool by the window and watching the foot traffic hustle by.

Antica Trattoria da Nino
salizada Seriman, 4858

Every once in a while, we all need a port in a storm, and this little trattoria is just that. It is certainly nothing to write home about and not worth a special trip, but if you are en route to take the boat to Murano and need a little sustenance, this is an inexpensive answer. The key is to remember where you are and not to expect gourmet renderings from a sophisticated chef. Order what can be prepared at the moment and you will do fine.

The knotty pine interior is filled with a collection of this and that, ranging from soccer scarves, framed sailor's knots, old Venetian prints, plastic plants, and assorted posters. The best Cheap Eat is the simple *menù turistico*. Start with the *spaghetti bolognese* and order either the mixed fish fry or the filet of sole for the main course. The vegetables are frozen or, worse yet, canned and really awful. Instead, order a mixed salad and for dessert a dish of ice cream. With a quarter liter of house *vino*, you will have had a filling meal and be out the door and on your way without putting major dents in your budget.

Bella Venezia
lista di Spagna, 129

The areas around most train stations are gastronomic wastelands filled with either cheap joints serving nearly inedible food, or overpriced tourist traps geared to squeezing diners for as much as possible because they know they will never be back. Bella Venezia is a bright spot in this touristy strip of real estate leading from the train station on lista di Spagna. Owner Armando Raccanello is on hand daily, keeping an eagle eye on everything from the bus boy to the chef and his kitchen staff. Specializing in fresh fish, Bella Venezia offers a time-honored combination of food that is well cooked, generously served, and affordable. The pink interior of the restaurant is delightful, with bouquets of flowers, candles on the tables, and pictures of old Venice on the walls. White-coated waiters help with menu selections, pointing out specials and seasonal favorites.

The hot mixed-vegetable *antipasti* or the gratin of black mussels, clams, and scallops flavored with Cognac ushers in a memorable meal. In autumn and spring, the spider crabs or the fish soup with shellfish and white fish is another marvelous beginning. Still more fish specialties include the *tagliolini* with shrimp, spaghetti with lobster sauce, and fresh salmon or sole. Carnivores will love the beef filet pan-fried in butter and topped with a cream sauce made with Gorgonzola cheese. Rich and fattening, yes, but oh, so good! After concentrating on the rest of the meal, the best dessert will be the house zabaglione or a dish of *gelato*.

HOURS
Lunch 11:30 A.M.–3 P.M., dinner 6:30–10:30 P.M.

RESERVATIONS
Advised on holidays

CREDIT CARDS
AMEX, DC, MC, V

À LA CARTE
L 35,000, beverage not included

MENÙ TURISTICO
L 22,000, 3 courses, beverage not included; summer menù turistico, 2 courses and vegetable, beverage not included

ENGLISH
Yes

COVER & SERVICE CHARGES
L 3,000 cover, no service charge

Ca' d'Oro
calle del Pistor and ramo Ca' d'Oro, 3912–3952 (off strada Nuova)

Known by all its loyalists as "La Vedova," the Ca' d'Oro has been in the same family for 120 years. Judging from the inside, very little has changed in that time. Now it is run by Lorenzo, his sister Mirella, and Beppi, the waiter who knows everyone. The two rooms are filled with what looks like original furniture, with a marvelous collection of old copper pots hanging from the ceiling, and pretty antique white shaded lights. Anytime you go you will see an interesting sampling of area regulars sitting at the plain wooden tables, sharing a bottle of *vino rosso* and arguing about Sunday's soccer scores or the latest political scandal.

This is a handy place to keep in mind for a light lunch or dinner. There is no menu, and you won't be served any dessert. Everyone depends on Beppi to tell

AREA
Cannaregio

TELEPHONE
52.85.324

OPEN
Mon–Wed, Fri–Sat lunch and dinner

CLOSED
Sun; Thurs; Aug–2nd week Sept

HOURS
Lunch 12:30–3 P.M., dinner 7–10:30 P.M.

RESERVATIONS
Not necessary

CREDIT CARDS
None

À LA CARTE
L 12,000–25,000

MENÙ TURISTICO
None

what the chef has prepared that day—maybe a tripe soup, pasta with seafood, or a hearty stew. You can have a bowl of the soup and a made-to-order sandwich, or mix and match a plate of their *antipasti*, which are displayed on a marble counter by the entrance. Service has been known to be cool, but after a drink or two, your Italian should improve and you will feel more at home.

Da Bepi
salizzada D. Pistor, 4550

AREA
Cannaregio
TELEPHONE
52.85.031
OPEN
Wed–Mon lunch and dinner
CLOSED
Tues; Jan–Feb 7 (depending on Carnival)
HOURS
Lunch noon–3 P.M., dinner 7–10 P.M.
RESERVATIONS
Suggested for weekends
CREDIT CARDS
DC, MC, V
À LA CARTE
L 26,000, beverage not included
MENÙ TURISTICO
L 25,000, 3 courses, beverage included; available in summer only
ENGLISH
Yes
COVER & SERVICE CHARGES
L 2,500 cover, no service charge

One hundred years ago this was a rough-and-ready watering hole for the workers who cleaned the canals. Today, only the beamed ceiling remains as a reminder of those rowdy days. Inside this modest little trattoria near Ca' d'Oro are two wood-paneled rooms with the usual paintings of Venice hanging about. In front is a shaded patio perfect for combining warm-weather dining with the sport of people-watching. The food at Da Bepi is good because the chef creatively interprets traditional Venetian home cooking while keeping the prices within reason. Daily specials depend on the season, but you can always expect to find *baccalà* (creamed salted cod), marinated sardines, liver with onions and polenta, and wonderful homemade desserts, especially the chocolate almond cake with creamy chocolate frosting. The pastas are served in generous portions with lots of crusty bread on the side for lapping up the last drop of delicious sauce. A set menu for L 25,000 that includes three courses and the wine is available only during the summer months.

Il Melograno
calle Riello, 458B

AREA
Cannaregio
TELEPHONE
52.42.553
OPEN
Tues–Sun lunch
CLOSED
Sun dinner; Mon; Nov or Dec

Understated elegance characterizes this handsome restaurant well off the tourist circuit in Cannaregio. The sophisticated interior in its utter simplicity reflects owner Massimiliano Bico's interest in art and appreciation of fine food. A specially designed Murano mirror, framed by two original Mirós, underscores the pomegranate (melograno) motif carried throughout the restaurant.

Several years ago Sr. Bico hired Adriana, a talented and award-winning chef who studied at Le Nôtre in Paris. Her refined cuisine is a beautiful match for the restaurant's lovely atmosphere. Prices are more special occasion and celebration than casual night out, and, from appetizers to desserts, there is plenty to celebrate. As with all fine restaurants, the menu changes and reflects the best of the seasonal offerings. You might start with grilled cheese and mushrooms or venison ham marinated with fresh herbs, then go on to the fettuccine tossed with chunks of tomato and a handful of basil or the spaghetti with fresh clams in the shell. When ordering, be sure to consult the list of the chef's specialties, many of which are creative variations of Venetian standards. These include fresh sardines mixed with onions, cuttlefish in black ink sauce with polenta, and stewed salt cod. Special requests are honored in case you don't see something on the menu that appeals. It is important to save room for one of the desserts, especially the rich cheesecake or, for a lighter ending, a scoop of the chocolate truffle ice cream. Service at Il Melograno is professional and efficient, the mix of diners, especially at lunch, is attractive, and the quality of everything served is uniformly high. Almost everyone who has eaten here once returns. I know I did, and I hope you will too.

HOURS
Lunch 12:30–2 P.M., dinner 7:30–9 P.M.

RESERVATIONS
Suggested for both lunch and dinner

CREDIT CARDS
AMEX, MC, V

À LA CARTE
L 50,000, beverage included

MENÙ TURISTICO
None

ENGLISH
Yes

COVER & SERVICE CHARGES
L 3,500 cover, no service charge

Ristorante al Ponte
rio Terra alla Maddalena, 2352

For decent dining, the farther you can get from the train station in almost any city, the better off you will be. Ristorante al Ponte is within easy walking distance to the *ferrovia* (railway station), but just far enough away to elude the touristy dining nightmare that surrounds it. This is a quiet spot, tucked next to a bridge along the rio Terra alla Maddalena. The service by uniformed waiters is dignified and formal. The lighting is subdued and the tables well spaced, making

AREA
Cannaregio

TELEPHONE
72.07.044

OPEN
Wed–Mon lunch and dinner

CLOSED
Tues; June or July

HOURS
Lunch 12:30–2:30 P.M., dinner 6:30–10 P.M.

this restaurant a favorite with first-time visitors and romantics alike. The impressive *antipasti* display of salad fixings and tempting appetizers tells you good things are ahead. The pastas concentrate on fish, with sauces made from tuna, crab, shrimp, and cuttlefish. Always ask what is fresh that day, because they do serve some frozen fish. If you are having meat, the tender veal scallop with lemon, and the filet steak in wine sauce are two solid choices. For the vegetable garnish, I like the grilled red chicory or the mixed vegetables vinaigrette. Desserts are from a local bakery and really quite good, but there is always a nice selection of fresh fruit and excellent cheeses if you don't want a high-calorie finish.

RESTAURANTS IN CASTELLO

Al Covo
Cip Ciap
Trattoria Rivetta
Trattoria Tofanelli

Al Covo
campiello della Pescaria, 3968

AREA
Castello

TELEPHONE
52.23.812

OPEN
Fri–Tues lunch and dinner

CLOSED
Wed; Thurs; Aug 1–15, Jan

HOURS
Lunch 12:45–2:15 P.M.,
dinner 7:30–10:15 P.M.

RESERVATIONS
Essential for dinner and holidays

CREDIT CARDS
chef's , DC, MC, V

À LA CARTE
L 60,000, beverage not included

MENÙ TURISTICO
None

If I could eat only one fine meal in Venice, Al Covo would definitely be one of my top choices. It was opened in 1987 by Diane and Cesare Benelli, a dynamic American/Italian couple who know and appreciate good food. The popularity of Al Covo is due to the excellence of its cuisine, prepared by Cesare, a talented and creative chef, and the cozy, warm atmosphere created by Diane using their collection of antiques and local artwork. Fresh flowers and candles adorn the tables, which are formally set with floral-patterned china, heavy cutlery, and nice crystal. While looking over the menu, a glass of complimentary champagne and some bite-sized nibbles are brought to your table. The assorted breads are served with iced butter curls, a treat unknown in most of Venice. If you love seafood and feel like splurging a little more, order the assorted seafood appetizer for two. There

The sidebar for the first restaurant (top of page):

RESERVATIONS
Advised

CREDIT CARDS
AMEX, MC, V

À LA CARTE
L 28,000, beverage not included

MENÙ TURISTICO
L 14,000, 3 course, beverage not included

ENGLISH
Enough

COVER & SERVICE CHARGES
L 3,000 cover; 12% service charge

are seven or eight mini-tastes of fish and shellfish fixed in unusual ways, each served separately to better savor the flavor of each. If this doesn't appeal, consider the dried codfish with polenta or the local clams sautéed with fresh ginger. As a pasta course, try the daily special or the fettuccine with fresh tomato and basil, based on a recipe from Cesare's grandmother. For the main course, the platter of mixed local fish served with fried zucchini or artichokes, or the grilled Aberdeen steak are sure-fire winners. So is the boned quail *al diavolo* served with wild rice. It is imperative that you save room for one of Diane's divine desserts. The choices are endless: chocolate chip and oatmeal cookies to dip in sweet wine, a bitter chocolate cake to behold, and a pear and prune cake with grappa sauce.

Service by the English-speaking staff is attentive and helpful. Prices are not for budgeteers, so reserve this special meal for a last night in Venice with someone you love.

Note: Al Covo is a member of the Ristoranti della Buona Accoglienza. See Ai Gondolieri, page 114, for details.

Cip Ciap
calle del Mondo Nuovo, 5799

If you want a slice of pizza, a bulging calzone (stuffed pizza) or an assortment of small pizzas for a quick snack, don't miss this busy little establishment off the campo Santa Maria Formosa. This is Italian fast food served with gusto and made while you wait and watch. You can eat here, standing up, or have your food packaged and take it with you. Dole out a worthwhile L 2,000 (and up) per slice of pizza and a little more for the calzone and take your feast over to the campo Santa Maria Formosa, sit on a bench, and watch the world parade by. It is a perfect way to feel very Italian and have a satisfying Cheap Eat in the bargain.

ENGLISH
Yes
COVER & SERVICE CHARGES
L 4,000 cover, no service charge

AREA
Castello at Ponte del Mondo Nuovo
TELEPHONE
52.36.621
OPEN
Thurs-Tues
CLOSED
Wed; NAC
HOURS
9 A.M.–9 P.M., continuous service
RESERVATIONS
Not accepted
CREDIT CARDS
None
À LA CARTE
L 2,000 and up, beverage not included
MENÙ TURISTICO
None
ENGLISH
Yes
COVER & SERVICE CHARGES
No cover or service charge

Trattoria Rivetta
campo SS. Filipino e Giacomo, 4625

AREA
Castello

TELEPHONE
52.87.302

OPEN
Tues–Sun, continuous service

CLOSED
Mon; Aug

HOURS
10 A.M.–10 P.M., continuous service

RESERVATIONS
Not necessary

CREDIT CARDS
None

À LA CARTE
L 30,000, beverage not included

MENÙ TURISTICO
None

ENGLISH
Yes

COVER & SERVICE CHARGES
L 1,500, no service charge

Trattoria Rivetta, squeezed in on the right side just before the Ponte San Provolo, is a genuine and reasonable alternative to the tourist traps that plague this area of Venice. A good sign, as always, is that the locals know about it and eat here in droves. You will see everyone from gondoliers on their breaks to women out for a gossipy afternoon with their friends. The menu is printed in English, and the restaurant serves full meals from 10 A.M. until 10 P.M., two distinct advantages for Venice visitors.

Portions are not for the light eater. In fact, the bowl of mussels ordered as a first course will be plenty if you add a salad and the fresh bread that always comes with every Italian meal. Growing boys and other hungry diners can start with *tagliolini ai granchio*, pasta with fresh crab, or a time-honored spaghetti with meat sauce. The squid cooked in its own black ink and served with polenta, and the jumbo grilled shrimp are delicious entrées. There is also a full line of meats including Venetian liver and onions, veal chops, and boiled beef with pesto sauce. Desserts are run-of-the-mill except for the house *tiramisù*, that heavenly rum-spiked cake layered with triple-cream cheese and dusted with chocolate.

Trattoria Tofanelli
rio Terra Garibaldi, 1650

AREA
Castello

TELEPHONE
52.35.722

OPEN
Thurs–Tues lunch and dinner

CLOSED
Wed; Nov through Jan

HOURS
Lunch noon–2:30 P.M., dinner 6:30–9 P.M.

RESERVATIONS
Not accepted

For as long as anyone can remember, sisters Nella and Micole Tofanelli have been serving their homespun food to the faithful in this nontouristy stretch of Venice about twenty minutes east of Saint Mark's Square. The trattoria is as old as the hills, but tidy and appealing in its own way. Inside are eight tables covered with brown and white tablecloths, an old icebox in one corner, and green plants sitting everywhere. If weather permits, try to sit outside along the rio Terra Garibaldi, where you can see and almost feel a part of the Venetian neighborhood life as it surges by. The small handwritten menu features meat and pasta, with fresh fish making only a cameo appearance. The sisters are best known for their *bigoli*—fresh egg pasta with anchovies and salsa—and veal scaloppine in Marsala sauce. None of the food hits the high notes of gourmet cuisine, but it is filling and the portions are ample. The best part is that the prices are about as old-fashioned as the setting, a real plus for any Cheap Eater in Venice.

Note: The sisters also operate a small hotel in connection with the restaurant. See *Cheap Sleeps in Italy*, page 130, for details.

RESTAURANTS IN DORSODURO
Ai Cugnai
Ai Gondolieri
Antica Locanda Montin
Antico Capon
Crepizza
Friggitoria da Bruno
Gelati Nico
Il Doge Gelaterie
L'Incontro
Taverna San Trovaso
Tonolo

Ai Cugnai
San Vio, 857

Those in search of a Cheap Eat near the Peggy Guggenheim Museum would do well to eat at Ai Cugnai. This cheapie, not too far from the Accademia vaporetto stop, has been run for almost forty years by three sisters and their families. Elegant it is not, but the cheerful, down-home atmosphere makes for an authentic Venetian experience. As you enter, you will find a cluster of neighbors standing at the bar comparing notes on their day. Eventually they will go on their way, or sit at one of the tables in back to have a meal. The food is far from fancy, but it is surprisingly good. If you want to keep your check in the budget department, then avoid the seafood. Instead go for their

CREDIT CARDS
None

À LA CARTE
L 20,000, beverage not included

MENÙ TURISTICO
None

ENGLISH
No

COVER & SERVICE CHARGES
L 700 cover, no service charge

AREA
Dorsoduro, near Accademia vaporetto stop

TELEPHONE
52.89.238

OPEN
Tues–Sun lunch and dinner

CLOSED
Mon; Aug 1–25

HOURS
Lunch noon–2:30 P.M., dinner 7–9:30 P.M.

RESERVATIONS
Not necessary

CREDIT CARDS
None

homemade *gnocchi*, the macaroni tossed with herbs and butter, or one of the soups. For the main course, the roast chicken, veal cutlet, or daily special is a reliable pick. Vegetables and salads are extra, as always, but not by much. Be sure to ask which of the vegetables are fresh; you don't want canned peas. For dessert, I wouldn't miss another piece of their velvety chocolate cake for anything, but if chocolate isn't your passion, try the almond cake—it is very special, too.

Ai Gondolieri
rio Terra San Vio, 366 (near Peggy Guggenheim Museum)

When reserving your table at Ai Gondolieri, ask to be in the main dining room, where you will sit at blue-linen-covered tables set with gleaming china and crystal, attractive silverware, fresh flowers, and glowing candles in the evening. The other narrow room off the bar has the same pretty place settings, but has uncomfortable wooden benches along the wall and serves as a corridor for restaurant patrons coming and going.

The food at Ai Gondolieri is more expensive than some, and that is why it should be saved for a Big Splurge on a special day or night. The best buy is definitely the *menù degustazione*, because it includes all of the chef's special dishes from appetizer to dessert. Coffee comes with it, but wine does not. You will start with three or four *antipasti* choices, including snails in Burgundy wine sauce, an unusual treatment of polenta cooked with smoky bacon, or a baby artichoke torte. Next will be a homemade pasta—perhaps early spring asparagus tossed with buttery egg noodles or tortellini with truffles. The main course might be a tender guinea hen garnished with seasonal vegetables, steak with mushrooms, or the chef's daily special. Wrapping it all up is a choice of such luscious homemade desserts as a strawberry cream cake, and warm apple pie lightly dusted with cinnamon.

À LA CARTE
L 24,000, beverage not included
MENÙ TURISTICO
None
ENGLISH
Limited
COVER & SERVICE CHARGES
L 2,000 cover, 10% service charge

AREA
Dorsoduro
TELEPHONE
52.86.396
OPEN
Wed–Mon lunch and dinner
CLOSED
Tues; 15 days in Aug (varies)
HOURS
Bar 9 A.M.–10 P.M., restaurant: lunch noon–2:45 P.M., dinner 8–10 P.M.
RESERVATIONS
Recommended, especially for dinner and Sun
CREDIT CARDS
AMEX, MC, V
À LA CARTE
L 50,000, beverage not included
MENÙ TURISTICO
L 45,000, 3 courses and coffee, wine extra
ENGLISH
Yes
COVER & SERVICE CHARGES
L 3,000 cover, 10% service charge

Note: This restaurant is part of a recently formed group of independent restaurateurs called Ristoranti della Buona Accoglienza. The organization pledges a proper price-to-quality ratio, the use of fine products, and quality service in an agreeable atmosphere. If you have any complaints about the food or service in any of the member restaurants, please call 52.39.896 or write to them at Casella Postale No. 624, 30100 Venezia, Italy. The other members listed in *Cheap Eats in Italy* are Al Covo, page 110, and Ignazio, page 131.

Antica Locanda Montin
fondamenta Eremite, 1147

Reservations are essential at this seventeenth-century inn, where the large dining room looks as if it has kept every piece of furniture and painting accumulated during the past forty-five years. The paintings were donated by or purchased from many renowned patrons, including Modigliani, Mark Rothko, Jackson Pollock, and virtually every artistic figure who has passed through Venice since the end of World War II. The arbor-covered garden in back is a popular warm-weather place to dine and to experience the real Venice.

Although the quality of food and service can be erratic, the chef's versions of the Venetian standards of marinated sardines, *spaghetti alle vongole* (with clams), *rigatoni ai quattro formaggi* (with four cheeses), liver with onions and polenta, and Adriatic fish either deep-fried or grilled are all wonderful. The desserts, so loaded with butter, cream, and sugar that they should carry health warnings, include a *semifreddo* with strawberries and a rich chocolate torte slathered in whipped cream.

Note: The Locanda also has hotel rooms. See *Cheap Sleeps in Italy*, page 135, for details.

AREA
Dorsodoro

TELEPHONE
52.27.151

OPEN
Thurs–Mon lunch and dinner, Tues lunch only

CLOSED
Tues dinner; Wed; Aug 1–10; Jan 1–20

HOURS
Lunch 12:30–2:30 P.M., dinner 7:30–10 P.M.

RESERVATIONS
Strongly recommended

CREDIT CARDS
AMEX, DC, MC, V

À LA CARTE
L 30,000, beverage not included

MENÙ TURISTICO
None

ENGLISH
Yes

COVER & SERVICE CHARGES
L 3,000 cover; 12% service charge

Antico Capon
campo Santa Margherita, 3004

AREA
Dorsoduro
TELEPHONE
52.85.252
OPEN
Thurs–Tues lunch and dinner
CLOSED
Wed; Nov
HOURS
Lunch noon–3 P.M.,
dinner 7–11 P.M.
RESERVATIONS
Not necessary
CREDIT CARDS
AMEX, DC, MC, V
À LA CARTE
L 4,000–11,000, pizzas,
beverage not included
MENÙ TURISTICO
L 16,000, 3 courses, beverage
not included
ENGLISH
Yes
COVER & SERVICE CHARGES
L 1,500 cover, 12% service charge

Ask Italians who know and love pizza and they will tell you that thin crusts are in, thick crusts are out, and the best pizzas are always wood-fired. Due to strict fire regulations and the usual morass of red tape connected with anything the Italians do, most of the pizzerias in Venice use electric ovens. The good news is that Antico Capon on campo Santa Margherita has a wood-fired pizza oven. Because of this, it is wildly popular with the natives, who think nothing of crossing the city for one of their wonderful pizzas. They know to ignore the regular menu, except for the prosciutto or a salad, and order one of the forty-one varieties of pizza. The choices range from a simple marinara with garlic and oregano, to one with everything from radicchio and shrimp to salmon, caviar, and cream. For dessert, go across the square and have a big cup of the creamy *gelato* at Il Doge Gelaterie (see page 117).

Crepizza
San Pantalon, 3757

AREA
Dorsoduro
TELEPHONE
52.29.189
OPEN
Wed–Mon lunch and dinner
CLOSED
Tues; 2 weeks mid-Aug
HOURS
Lunch noon–3:30 P.M.,
dinner 7–10:30 P.M.
RESERVATIONS
Yes
CREDIT CARDS
AMEX, DC, MC, V
À LA CARTE
L 20,000, beverage not
included
MENÙ TURISTICO
None

Crepizza is a busy hub for area residents, students from the nearby university, and stray hotel guests seeking lighter Italian fare. Both savory and sweet crepes, a dozen-plus pizzas, and a few pastas and meat dishes make up the menu. The crepes and pizzas always stay the same, but you never know what is likely to be on the regular menu because it changes every few days, depending on the availability of seasonal produce. The portions are small, so you can order a dinner and dessert crepe, or a pizza and a sweet crepe, and not feel totally stuffed. The best crepes are the *rustica* with cheese, mushrooms, ham, and béchamel sauce, and the *effimera*, with ricotta cheese and *prosciutto crudo*. Most of the desserts are the usual choices you see everywhere. I recommend ordering a dessert crepe, either the *fragolona* with ice cream, whipped cream, and fresh strawberries, or the *coccolona* with coconut, chocolate ice cream, and chocolate sauce.

The interior is light and open, with beamed ceilings, and dried flowers hanging in baskets on the beige walls. The service by overworked waiters is adequate, but uninspired. Reservations are accepted, and you should make them for evenings, when the restaurant is still filled to the brim at 9:30 or 10:00.

Friggitoria da Bruno
calle Lunga Santa Barnaba, 2754A

Friggitoria da Bruno has been serving budget-priced Venetian food longer than anyone cares to remember. The forty-nine seats in the two plain rooms are filled for lunch and dinner with pensioners, starving students, and anyone else on a hard-core budget safari in Venice. You will not find imaginative food preparation, any attempt at decor, or much service with a smile. All you will get is a filling meal with absolutely no ruffles or flourishes. There is a *menù turistico* that includes a first and second course with vegetable and wine included, but not the dessert or coffee. Another approach, if you are not ravenous, is to order just one course and a salad from the à la carte menu, sticking with the specials because you know they are the freshest items to come out of the kitchen. You can skip the fish because it is all frozen, and the desserts are packaged, so you do not need these either. The rough-and-ready house red or white wine is very low-priced. You can have a half liter here for what a glass would cost you at home.

Gelati Nico
Zattere, 922

The Zattere is the southernmost promenade in Venice and is especially popular with families who spend Sunday afternoons strolling along the walkway that borders the Giudecca Canal. There are other *gelaterie* on the Zattere, but Nico is far and away the best and most popular. I was here on a freezing April afternoon during a driving rainstorm, and there were

ENGLISH
Yes
COVER & SERVICE CHARGES
L 2,000 cover, 10% service charge

AREA
Dorsoduro
TELEPHONE
52.08.978
OPEN
Mon–Fri lunch and dinner
CLOSED
Sat; Sun; Aug 14–30, Dec 20–Jan 8
HOURS
Lunch noon–2:30 P.M., dinner 7:30–10 P.M., bar 9 A.M.–2:30 P.M. and 5–10 P.M.
RESERVATIONS
Not necessary
CREDIT CARDS
None
À LA CARTE
L 19,000, beverage not included
MENÙ TURISTICO
L 17,000, 2 courses and vegetable, beverage included
ENGLISH
Yes
COVER & SERVICE CHARGES
L 1,500 cover, no service charge

AREA
Dorsoduro
TELEPHONE
52.25.293
OPEN
Fri–Wed
CLOSED
Thurs; Dec 15–Jan 15
HOURS
7 A.M.–10 P.M.
RESERVATIONS
Not accepted
CREDIT CARDS
None

À LA CARTE
L 4,800 *gianduiotto*, others start
at L 4,800
MENÙ TURISTICO
None
ENGLISH
Yes
COVER & SERVICE CHARGES
None if you order to go;
L 1,500 cover to sit on deck by
canal, but no service charge

ten people ahead of me in line waiting to dig into their specialty, a *gianduiotto*: a large slice of dense chocolate hazelnut ice cream buried in whipped cream and served in a cup to have there, or to go. Others have tried to imitate it, but have never equalled this version. There are other ice cream treats available, from sundaes to frappés, but about the only thing anyone orders here is the famous *gianduiotto*.

Il Doge Gelaterie
campo Santa Margherita, 3058A

AREA
Dorsoduro
TELEPHONE
None
OPEN
Daily in summer, Tues–Sun in winter
CLOSED
Mon in winter; Nov through Jan
HOURS
10 A.M.–8 P.M. in winter,
9 A.M.–1 A.M. in summer
RESERVATIONS
Not accepted
CREDIT CARDS
None
À LA CARTE
L 2,000 and up
MENÙ TURISTICO
None
ENGLISH
Some
COVER & SERVICE CHARGES
None

I must confess I adore Italian *gelato*. Nowhere in Venice is it any better than at Il Doge Gelaterie, a shrine to this scrumptious treat located on the campo Santa Margherita. All the ice cream is made here by Giovanni Grazziella and his family. He has more than forty-seven superb flavors in his repertoire, including rum, Amaretto, *marron glacé*, *tiramisù*, and English trifle. He also makes countless fruit sorbets and, to keep insistent dieters happy, several low-fat yogurts. However, there is one flavor you absolutely cannot miss, and that is his special *panna cotta del Doge*, a custard-based ice cream swirled with ribbons of caramel. It sounds rather pedestrian, but let me assure you, after one taste you will agree that it is anything but. Just thinking about it makes me wish I were on my way right now to have another scoop or two of this celestial ice cream.

L'Incontro
rio Terra Canal (Ponte dei Pugni), campo Santa Margherita 3062A

AREA
Dorsoduro
TELEPHONE
52.22.404
OPEN
Tues–Sun lunch and dinner
CLOSED
Mon; July
HOURS
Lunch 12:30–3 P.M.,
dinner 7:30–11 P.M.

L'Incontro is just the kind of place you always hope will be just around the corner, and it was for me. While doing the research for the Venice portion of *Cheap Eats in Italy* and *Cheap Sleeps in Italy*, I lived on campo Squellini, near the campo Santa Margherita in Dorsoduro. Naturally I tried every Cheap Eat candidate in the vicinity, and L'Incontro tops my list of favorites. I like it because it is local and extremely popular, it serves dependable, well-priced food, and it is or was until now, totally undiscovered. It is also impossible to locate unless you have some specific guidelines, because there is no sign or indication outside that this is a restaurant. (See below for detailed instructions on finding it.)

The small restaurant is composed of two rooms, with a bar dividing them. The low beamed ceilings, lacy window curtains, flowered tablecloths, baskets on the walls, and straw flower arrangements scattered throughout create a cozy, old-world atmosphere. If you go for dinner, give it a chance to fill up with other diners and arrive about 8:30 or 9:00 P.M. When planning your meal, forget the long printed menu and stay strictly with the handwritten daily one. These imaginative specials include generous servings of homemade pastas with fresh herbs and vegetables, and unusual *gnocchi* filled with olive paste or saffron-scented mushrooms. The chef does not prepare any fish, but concentrates instead on wild game in season, and grilled, roasted, or stewed beef and pork. The desserts are adequate, but not thrilling, probably because they are made elsewhere, so I always passed on the sweet course. The house wine is light and refreshing.

How to find L'Incontro: The address is rio Terra Canal, 3062A. This is toward the left end of campo Santa Margherita as you head to campo Santa Barnaba and the floating vegetable market. At lunch and dinner time you will see the daily menu taped to a small window to the left of the door. The restaurant is next to a mask shop. When all else fails, ask a shopkeeper—everyone knows it.

RESERVATIONS
Advised for both lunch and dinner

CREDIT CARDS
MC, V

À LA CARTE
L 25,000, beverage not included

MENÙ TURISTICO
None

ENGLISH
Yes

COVER & SERVICE CHARGES
L 3,000 cover, no service charge

Taverna San Trovaso
fondamenta Priuli, 1018

The Taverna San Trovaso is small and very popular. You *must* call ahead for reservations and arrive on time if you expect to get a table.

Venetians know and recommend it as a restaurant where a good, uncomplicated meal can be had for a moderate price. Restful and relaxing it is not, but typical, full of happy locals busy having a good time

AREA
Dorsoduro

TELEPHONE
52.03.703

OPEN
Tues–Sun lunch and dinner

CLOSED
Mon, Dec 31–Jan 2

HOURS
Lunch noon–3 P.M., dinner 7–10 P.M.

RESERVATIONS
Essential; table held 10 minutes

CREDIT CARDS
AMEX, DC, MC, V

À LA CARTE
L 28,500, beverage not included
MENÙ TURISTICO
L 20,000, 3 courses, beverage included
ENGLISH
Yes
COVER & SERVICE CHARGES
L 2,000 cover, no service charge

and raising the noise level by the minute it is.

The *menù turistico* is a good value and offers enough choices not to be boring. The à la carte menu is varied and includes pizzas at night, so it should appeal to everyone. Servings are tremendous, thus it is imperative to arrive hungry in order to do justice to it all.

Tonolo
salizzada San Pantalon, 3764

AREA
Dorsoduro
TELEPHONE
52.37.209
OPEN
Tues–Sun
CLOSED
Mon; 10 days in Aug (varies)
HOURS
8 A.M.–9 P.M.
RESERVATIONS
Not accepted
CREDIT CARDS
None
À LA CARTE
L 2,000 and up for cappuccino and pastry
MENÙ TURISTICO
None
ENGLISH
No
COVER & SERVICE CHARGES
No cover, no service charge

You will undoubtedly be the only tourist when you join students, dowagers with blue hair, and well-dressed businessmen and shopkeepers at Tonolo, the most popular place to have a cappuccino and pastry in the San Pantalon area of Venice. Before arriving, sharpen your elbows and determination to better edge your way to the counter where the young women miraculously take orders as they are shouted and somehow keep them all straight. Open from 8 in the morning until 9 at night, this constantly crowded bakery makes some of the best high-calorie treats in Venice, and everyone knows it. In the morning, indulge in a fresh cream-filled doughnut, a plain or almond *cornetto* (croissant), raisin pound cake, or a buttery brioche. At lunch, try two or three little pizzas or a slice of quiche. In the late afternoon, any one of their indulgent pastries or glorious cakes will make you even happier that you are in Venice.

Note: There are no tables. You must eat standing up or have your order packaged to go.

RESTAURANTS IN SAN MARCO
Bora Bora
Da Nico
Fiore
Leon Bianco
Osteria ai Assassini
Paolin
Premiata Latteria Zorzi
Rosticceria S. Bartolomeo
Sempione

Bora Bora
calle dei Stagneri della Fava, 5251 (near Rialto Bridge)

Pizza, pizza, and more pizza is what you will find at Bora Bora, the Venetian Baskin Robbins of pizza, with more than forty-one types listed on the menu. Since its opening a few years ago, it has become popular with a youthfully glamorous crowd who gravitates here for the good food and bright Polynesian atmosphere.

Don't let the silly names of some of the pizzas turn you off. For example, the Gorgo Speck, with tomato, Gorgonzola cheese, and *speck* (ham), and the Ali Baba, with cheese, mushrooms, onions, sausage, and sesame seeds, are both delicious. Dieters need not worry; there is even a low-cal pizza topped with tomato, hearts of palm, and corn. Also on the menu are several large salads filled with seafood or vegetables. If pizza doesn't hit the spot, maybe one of their three crepes or seven made-to-order pastas will. It is hard to imagine considering dessert, and since nothing is made here, you probably should not.

AREA
San Marco
TELEPHONE
52.36.583
OPEN
Thurs-Tues lunch and dinner
CLOSED
Wed; July 1–15; Jan 15–31
HOURS
Lunch noon–3 P.M.
dinner 7–10:30 P.M.
RESERVATIONS
Not necessary
CREDIT CARDS
None
À LA CARTE
Pizzas from L 5,000–12,000, beverage not included
MENÙ TURISTICO
None
ENGLISH
Yes
COVER & SERVICE CHARGES
L 500 per pizza to take out

Da Nico
frezzeria, 1702

Da Nico, not too far from piazza San Marco, is always crowded early in the evening with regulars who show up with their families for the simple, well-prepared traditional *cucina* offered by owner Donato. It is a comfortable restaurant, with salmon-colored tablecloths, half-wood walls, bright lights, and abstract paintings. The waiters are serious and helpful, and the welcome offered by Lionella, Donato's pretty daughter, is always friendly.

Among the first-course homemade pastas, the popular favorite is the *tagliatelle alla boscaiuola*, a subtle interplay of mushrooms, tomatoes, and smoky bacon with a light dusting of freshly grated Parmesan cheese. Fish fanciers will be pleased to find Adriatic sole lightly cooked in butter; grilled scampi; and a platter of fried fish. Meat eaters will be happy with the

AREA
San Marco
TELEPHONE
52.21.543
OPEN
Tues–Sun lunch and dinner
CLOSED
Mon; Aug 1–15
HOURS
Lunch noon–2:30 P.M., dinner 7–10:30 P.M.
RESERVATIONS
Advised for dinner
CREDIT CARDS
AMEX, DC, MC, V
À LA CARTE
L 45,000, beverage not included
MENÙ TURISTICO
None

ENGLISH
Yes

COVER & SERVICE CHARGES
L 3,000 cover; 12% service

sautéed calves' kidneys or the *petto di pollo alla Nico*, a breast of chicken served in a light mushroom sauce and garnished with steamed vegetables. For dessert, either the fresh fruit tart or the delicious nut cake is the best ending.

Note: Prices here nudge toward the Big Splurge category, so unless your budget is flexible, reserve a table here for a last-night dinner or another special occasion.

Fiore
calle delle Botteghe, 3460–61 (off campo San Stefano)

AREA
San Marco

TELEPHONE
52.35.310

OPEN
Wed–Mon lunch and dinner

CLOSED
Tues; Jan 15–Feb 5 (varies)

HOURS
Lunch noon–3 P.M.,
dinner 7–10 P.M.

RESERVATIONS
Definitely

CREDIT CARDS
AMEX, DC, MC, V

À LA CARTE
L 50,000, beverage not
included

MENÙ TURISTICO
None

ENGLISH
Yes

COVER & SERVICE CHARGES
L 3,000 cover, no service charge

I found Fiore while checking a hotel for *Cheap Sleeps in Italy*. I asked the hotel owner where he would take that special person in his life to celebrate, and without hesitation he said he always goes to Fiore, which is just a few minutes away.

Sergio Boschian has been at the helm of this charming contemporary restaurant for over ten years. During that time he has built a repeat clientele intent on having good food and good value in attractive surroundings. The seating is for only fifty diners, allowing the staff to give careful attention to each table. As with many restaurants in Venice, fish is the specialty of the house, and the chef is superb at turning out the most classic of dishes with finesse. If you are lucky enough to be here in early April or November, try the soft-shell crabs, a delicacy you must have if you like crab. A prizewinning appetizer almost anytime is the huge bowl of mussels liberally laced with garlic. For the pasta course, try *pennette alla Fiore*: tube pasta gently tossed with eggplant, tomato, assorted peppers, zucchini, and a splash of olive oil. The grilled fresh tuna, king scampi, and salmon are just three of the outstanding main-course plates you can enjoy. The desserts are sublime, particularly the chocolate truffle ice cream, and the heavenly lemon cake filled with cream and dusted with nuts. Because prices are on the high side, I reserve this for dining with someone very important to me.

Note: For an upscale neighborhood snack, drop into Fiore's adjacent bar and have a plate of savory *cicchetti*. The meatballs made with ground beef, potato, and parsley are wonderful. So are the fried zucchini, stuffed tomatoes, and cauliflower.

Leon Bianco
salizzada San Luca, 4153 (between campo San Luca and campo Manin)

When you want a snack or light meal and cannot face another street pizza, try Leon Bianco, the type of place Venetians patronize day after day. Terrific *cicchetti* (snacks) and *tramezzini* (sandwiches) are served throughout the day, but hot food is offered only between noon and 3 P.M. Rice or cheese croquettes, grilled shrimp, and roasted vegetables are only a few of the *cicchetti* you can pluck with a toothpick. There are always two or three hot dishes, and if you want to sample more than one, they will serve half portions. The *tramezzini*—served on toasted or plain bread filled with prosciutto, *funghi* (mushrooms), tomatoes, tuna, egg, shrimp, roast beef, or pork—were some of the best I tried in Venice. You can stand at the marble counters and rub shoulders with shopkeepers and businessmen, or, if you want to take a more relaxed approach to your meal, you can sit in the back room and still not have any service or cover charge added to your bill.

AREA
San Marco
TELEPHONE
52.21.180
OPEN
Mon–Sat
CLOSED
Sun; NAC
HOURS
Snacks 8 A.M.–8 P.M., hot food noon–3 P.M.
RESERVATIONS
Not accepted
CREDIT CARDS
None
À LA CARTE
L 1,000 and up for *cicchetti*, L 1,500 and up for *tramezzini*, L 4,000 and up for hot food
MENÙ TURISTICO
None
ENGLISH
Yes
COVER & SERVICE CHARGES
No cover or service charge

Osteria ai Assassini
rio Terra dei Assassini, 3695

For years this was only a place to buy wine by the bottle or case. Then Giuseppe Galardi turned it into an *enoteca* (wine bar) that has enjoyed a growing popularity with the locals, probably because they are the only ones who can find it.

Actually, you can find it—if you have an abundance of determination and patience and are armed with the best street map of Venice money can buy. To make things even more difficult, there is no name outside. Just look for the yellow light over the door,

AREA
San Marco
TELEPHONE
52.87.986
OPEN
Mon–Fri lunch and evening snacks, Sat evening snacks
CLOSED
Sat lunch; Sun; Aug; 2 weeks at Christmas
HOURS
Lunch 11:30 A.M.–3 P.M., snacks 7–11 P.M.

RESERVATIONS
Not necessary
CREDIT CARDS
None
À LA CARTE
L 3,000 and up for *cicchetti*,
L 6,000 and up for lunch;
beverage not included
MENÙ TURISTICO
None
ENGLISH
Yes
COVER & SERVICE CHARGES
No cover or service charge

which is turned on when the place is open.

Every day the long wooden tables and hard benches are filled with people having lunch or *cicchetti* and sipping some of the four hundred wines that are always available. *Cicchetti* are little snacks similar to Spanish tapas, ranging from a piece of bread with a slice of prosciutto to meatballs, grilled vegetables, and deep-fried zucchini flowers, to whipped salt cod and marinated sardines. For many, a few *cicchetti* to nibble on and a glass or two of nice wine can easily substitute for lunch or a light supper. At lunch the menu offers three or four appetizers, several main courses, and daily specials. Tuesday and Friday, fresh fish is served. *Bollito misto*—boiled meat—is the Thursday special and, on Wednesday, there is a creamy *pasta e fagioli*. The only dessert is biscotti dipped in sweet wine.

Paolin
campo S. Stefano, 2962

AREA
San Marco
TELEPHONE
52.23.576
OPEN
Tues–Sun
CLOSED
Mon; Dec 15–31; Jan
HOURS
Winter 8 A.M.–9 P.M.,
summer 8 A.M.–midnight
RESERVATIONS
Not accepted
CREDIT CARDS
None
À LA CARTE
L 2,000 and up for cones
MENÙ TURISTICO
None
ENGLISH
Yes
COVER & SERVICE CHARGES
L 1,000 cover for tables, no
service charge

Paolin is considered by many to make the best ice cream in Venice. Certainly the hazelnut is amazing, and so is the pistachio and the extra-strength coffee gelato. The shop has recently been redone, but is still a high-concept hangout, with outdoor tables offering ringside seating for some of the best people-watching in the city. Even though it offers less than fifteen flavors, Paolin is a full-service ice cream parlor where you can stand, sit inside or out, or take your *gelato* with you. Best of all, everything is produced by hand on the premises and is simply delicious (except for the ready-made sandwiches and the dry cookies—these are quite forgettable). In summer you can stroll by until midnight for a *gelato*; the rest of the year, it is open until 9 P.M.

Premiata Latteria Zorzi
calle dei Fuseri, 4359

AREA
San Marco
TELEPHONE
52.25.350
OPEN
Mon–Sat

It looks like dozens of other bars selling dairy products, assorted sandwiches, and packaged goodies, but the difference is the dining room in back and another, larger one, upstairs with a no-smoking section. The downstairs dining is considered to be part of the bar, so there is no cover charge. Eating upstairs will add another L 1,000 cover charge per person to the bill. For anyone looking for lighter fare with light price tags to match, this is one answer. Billed as the only vegetarian restaurant in Venice, here you will find office workers, young mothers with their babies in tow, and students eating *crostini* (toasted bread with different toppings); spinach crepes; vegetable platters with warm *scamorza* cheese; risotto with vegetables, stuffed peppers, or zucchini; and lovely salads. Freshly squeezed juices and toasted sandwiches are served continuously, but hot food is prepared only at lunchtime.

CLOSED
Sun; Aug
HOURS
Bar 7:30 A.M.–8:30 P.M.,
lunch noon–3:30 P.M.
RESERVATIONS
Not accepted
CREDIT CARDS
None
À LA CARTE
L 5,000 and up for lunch,
L 1,500 and up for sandwiches,
beverage not included
MENÙ TURISTICO
None
ENGLISH
Some
COVER & SERVICE CHARGES
L 1,000 cover to sit upstairs
MISCELLANEOUS
No smoking allowed

Rosticceria S. Bartolomeo
calle della Bissa, 5424 (off campo S. Bartolomeo, near the Rialto Bridge)

Cheap Eaters do not go to the upstairs restaurant here. Instead they go downstairs, through the self-service line, and take their food to one of the long tables by the window, thus avoiding the cover, service, and higher prices charged for almost the same food served upstairs. The downstairs snack bar is a popular refueling stop for those who simply cannot face another prosciutto sandwich or pizza. Featured each day are good selections of salads, pastas, and hot dishes that include the Venetian specialties of *baccalà alla Vicentina* (salt cod simmered in milk and herbs), deep-fried mozzarella, *seppie con polenta* (squid in black sauce), and all the usual desserts.

For L 15,000 or so, you will get a two- or three-course meal and a glass of house wine, and in Venice, this is a Cheap Eat.

AREA
San Marco
TELEPHONE
52.23.569
OPEN
Tues–Sun lunch and dinner
CLOSED
Mon; week before Carnival
HOURS
Lunch 10 A.M.–2:30 P.M.,
dinner 5–9 P.M.
RESERVATIONS
Not accepted
CREDIT CARDS
AMEX, DC, MC, V
À LA CARTE
L 15,000 beverage included;
L 4,500 and up per dish
MENÙ TURISTICO
None
ENGLISH
Enough
COVER & SERVICE CHARGES
No cover or service charge
downstairs

Sempione
Ponte Baretteri, 578

The beautiful canalside location, good service, and tempting Venetian cuisine draw me back to this restaurant time after time. Its privileged location near St. Mark's Square and some of the city's most luxurious

AREA
San Marco
TELEPHONE
52.26.022
OPEN
Wed–Mon lunch and dinner

CLOSED
Tues; Dec; Jan
HOURS
Lunch 11:30 A.M.–3 P.M.,
dinner 6:30–10 P.M.
RESERVATIONS
Advised for dinner
CREDIT CARDS
AMEX, MC, V
À LA CARTE
L 35,000, beverage not
included
MENÙ TURISTICO
None
ENGLISH
Yes
COVER & SERVICE CHARGES
L 2,500 cover, 12% service
charge

shops makes it an ideal stop for lunch or dinner. The best tables, naturally, are by the leaded windows overlooking the canal with gondolas quietly floating by. The food is simple, with unfussy preparations and a lavish use of olive oil. *Pennette* tossed with a sheer but well-flavored *amatriciana* sauce of tomatoes and sweet red peppers is a hit. So is the pasta with spider crab and the *spaghetti Sempione* with prawns, mussels, and octopus. It is tempting to finish every drop, but important to save room for the heaping platter of scampi and squid, or the cuttlefish in black ink sauce, served with polenta. Meat eaters will be pleased to find grilled liver and onions, steaks, veal dishes, and roast chicken. For a pleasant ending, *tiramisù* is presented in an agreeably light version. Because of Sempione's prime patch of real estate, prices are higher here. Unless you have an unlimited food budget, it is best to save this place for a modest splurge.

RESTAURANTS IN SAN POLO

Al Gobbo di Rialto
Aliani Gastronomia
Alla Madonna
All'Antico Pizzo
Al Milion
Caffè dei Frari
Cantina do Spade
Da Marco
Do Mori
Ignazio
Trattoria Pizzeria San Tomà

Al Gobbo di Rialto
ruga Rialto, 649

AREA
San Polo
TELEPHONE
52.04.603, 52.04.883
OPEN
Wed–Mon lunch and dinner
CLOSED
Tues; Jan 15–Feb 15

The talking birds Frederick and Cocco welcome you from their perches by the entrance of the covered garden terrace at this spacious *ristorante* near the Rialto Bridge. The welcome continues from the owner and staff, who make every effort to make first-time and regular guests feel equally at home and comfortable.

Start your meal by helping yourself from the bounty displayed at the *antipasti* table. Careful—you could easily make an entire meal out of the fish and vegetables that are so beautifully prepared and laid out. Any of the pasta dishes for two are guaranteed to please, and so is the fish soup, the rice scampi, and the huge serving of mussels and clams. Fresh sea bass, mixed sea grill, and sardines marinated and cooked with vinegar and onions are award-winning fish entrées, while succulent steaks, moist chicken, and tender veal capture the meat eaters' attention. The *torta di mandorle* (almond cake), and the fabulously rich chocolate cake are the chef's prize desserts, which everyone must try—even if it is only to share a bite. Getting out for under L 40,000 will require restraint, so you should consider your meal here a Big Splurge.

HOURS
Lunch noon–3 P.M., dinner 7–10 P.M.

RESERVATIONS
Not necessary

CREDIT CARDS
AMEX, DC, MC, V

À LA CARTE
L 45,000, beverage not included

MENÙ TURISTICO
None

ENGLISH
Yes

COVER & SERVICE CHARGES
L 3,000, 12% service charge

Aliani Gastronomia
ruga Vecchia S. Giovanni, 654–655

For fast, flavorful, and fabulous takeout deli-style food, the best and most central spot is Aliani Gastronomia near the Rialto Bridge. The shop, owned and operated by Bruno Aliani and his charming English-speaking wife, has been doing business in this location for thirty-six years, and only gets better with time. Fresh daily pastas (except on Monday), roast chicken, vegetables of the season, a wide variety of Italian cheeses and hams, fat sandwiches, and wines from Veneto keep the faithful coming back for more. Also available are packages of their hand-made dried pastas, the finest virgin olive oils, and tempting desserts from their bakery next door at no. 603. There are no tables for dining here, so plan on taking your picnic with you and enjoying it elsewhere.

AREA
San Polo (on main street leading to Rialto Bridge)

TELEPHONE
52.24.913

OPEN
Mon–Sat

CLOSED
Mon morning; Sun; Aug

HOURS
Tues–Sat 8 A.M.–1 P.M. and 5–7:30 P.M., Mon 5–7:30 P.M.

RESERVATIONS
Not accepted

CREDIT CARDS
None

À LA CARTE
L 4,000 and up

MENÙ TURISTICO
None

ENGLISH
Yes

COVER & SERVICE CHARGES
None

Alla Madonna
calle della Madonna, 594

Almost every guidebook on Venice lists Alla Madonna, and for good reasons. It is in a pivotal location on a narrow street on the San Polo side of the Rialto Bridge. The fresh fish is always delicious and reason-

AREA
San Polo (near Rialto Bridge)

TELEPHONE
52.23.824

OPEN
Thurs–Tues lunch and dinner
CLOSED
Wed; Aug 1–15, Dec 20–Jan 31
HOURS
Lunch noon–3 P.M.,
dinner 7–9:30 P.M.
RESERVATIONS
Essential for lunch and dinner
CREDIT CARDS
AMEX, MC, V
À LA CARTE
L 33,000, beverage not included
MENÙ TURISTICO
None
ENGLISH
Yes
COVER & SERVICE CHARGES
L 2,500 cover, 12% service charge

ably priced, and the atmosphere is typical and pleasing. The unadorned white tables are well spaced and filled every day with a good mix of chattering Venetians and visitors. If you arrive without reservations, you can expect to wait up to one hour for a table, so beware. Service by white-coated waiters, some of whom have been on the job since time began, can be brusque, but given the number of tables they have to serve, it is easy to see why patience can run thin during the crunch. From appetizer to pasta and main course, the star of the show is always fresh fish. As you enter, you will pass an iced display of just some of the many delicacies awaiting you. The specialties are seafood rice, spaghetti with black squid, squid with polenta, fried cuttlefish, mixed-fish fry, and grilled sole. Add a salad or fresh vegetable and a slice of Madonna cake (cream-filled sponge cake), and you will be in seventh heaven, or close to it.

All'Antico Pizzo
San Mateo, 814 (near Rialto Market)

AREA
San Polo
TELEPHONE
52.31.575
OPEN
Mon–Sat lunch and dinner, Sun lunch
CLOSED
Sun dinner; Mon; 15 days Jan and Aug (varies)
HOURS
Lunch 12:30–2:30 P.M.,
dinner 7:30–10 P.M.
RESERVATIONS
Not necessary
CREDIT CARDS
None
À LA CARTE
L 35,000, beverage not included
MENÙ TURISTICO
None

The Rialto fish and produce market is one of the must-sees of Venice. Today the old commercial meeting-place along the quay is a lively and colorful outdoor market crowded with countless stalls and shouting hawkers. Housewives and chefs come early each morning for the freshest seasonal food available, and tourists wander through eager to soak up the local color and take advantage of the many interesting photo opportunities. Whenever you are in this area, a good target for lunch is Antico Pizzo. The two knotty-pine rooms with simply laid tables are filled every day with regulars who come for the fine fish offered by Vittorio Marcolin and his two brothers Mario and Fabir. As you walk in, the fresh fish and *antipasti* display will tempt your tastebuds. Fish is number one here, prepared simply and without fanfare. Start with the fish risotto or a pasta with fresh seafood sauce. For the main course, I recommend the fried calamari or the squid with polenta. Always ask what the daily specials are because they are bound to be winners.

Landlubbers can settle for an omelette, liver with onions, or veal scaloppine fixed four different ways, but, frankly, the order of the day here should be fish. Desserts are not a high priority with the chef, so order a dish of seasonal fruit or a *gelato* to finish.

Al Milion
corte al Milion, San Giovanni Crisostomo, 5841

"We spoil our guests," says Mario, the longtime manager of Al Milion, a friendly *osteria* and trattoria that is reliably good, always busy and known and loved by almost everyone in Venice. You can join old-timers at the bar, or sit at one of the three tables by the bar and have a glass of good wine and a plate of *cicchetti* (snacks to munch on while drinking your wine), or, for a full meal, sit in the dining room at one of the tables covered with red-and-white-checked tablecloths with white paper overlays. Feel free to order as much or as little as you want, and if you do not see what you want on the handwritten menu, ask for it and chances are they can prepare it. Fish, cooked with skill and restraint, is the backbone of the main-course roster. There is salmon, squid in its own black ink sauce, and the ever-present mixed fried-fish platter. Other dishes that earn high marks are the *bigoli in salsa* (whole-wheat pasta with anchovy and onion sauce), roast veal, and the homemade desserts, especially the almond cake and *tiramisù*. You can't call for reservations because they don't take them, so to avoid a wait, arrive early during the meal service.

AREA
San Polo
TELEPHONE
52.29.302
OPEN
Thurs–Tues lunch and dinner
CLOSED
Wed; Aug
HOURS
Lunch 11 A.M.–2 P.M., dinner 6–10 P.M.
RESERVATIONS
Not accepted
CREDIT CARDS
None
À LA CARTE
L 32,000, beverage not included
MENÙ TURISTICO
None
ENGLISH
Yes
COVER & SERVICE CHARGES
L 2,000 cover, 10% service charge

Caffè dei Frari
fondamenta dei Frari, 2564 (foot of Ponte dei Frari after leaving campo dei Frari)

At this rambunctious caffè near the campo dei Frari, you will find yourself mixing with Venetian students, men quaffing a third glass of Chianti far too early in the day, and elderly women jump-starting their trip to the market with a caffè latte or cappuccino. There is always neighborly service and made-to-order savory sandwiches served from dawn

AREA
San Polo
TELEPHONE
52.41.877
OPEN
Mon–Sat
CLOSED
Sun; Aug
HOURS
Winter 7:30 A.M.–8:30 P.M., summer 7:30 A.M.–midnight

ENGLISH
Yes
COVER & SERVICE CHARGES
L 2,500 cover, no service charge

| | |

RESERVATIONS
Not accepted
CREDIT CARDS
None
À LA CARTE
L 6,000, beverage not included
MENÙ TURISTICO
None
ENGLISH
Yes
COVER & SERVICE CHARGES
None

to dusk by owner Giorgio and his casual crew. I like to go around noon and order a pocket-bread sandwich filled with slices of *prosciutto crudo* (air-dried salt-cured ham), and thin slices of provolone or *mozzarella di bufala* cheese.

For the best people-watching, sit downstairs at one of the six round tables along the padded banquette, or, in summer, at one of the tables outside facing the canal.

Cantina do Spade
calle do Spade, 860

AREA
San Polo
TELEPHONE
52.10.574
OPEN
Mon–Sat
CLOSED
Sun; Aug
HOURS
9 A.M.–2:30 P.M. and 4:30–8:30 P.M., lunch noon–2:30 P.M.
RESERVATIONS
Not accepted
CREDIT CARDS
None
À LA CARTE
L 5,000 daily specials, L 1,500 sandwiches, L 800 and up for snacks
MENÙ TURISTICO
None
ENGLISH
Enough
COVER & SERVICE CHARGES
L 300 cover for tables, no service charge

Cantina do Spade is almost lost in the Venetian labyrinth under the archways of the Do Spade bridge just south of the Rialto fishmarket. Don't look for a sign, because there isn't one. The two lanterns on each side of the entrance at No. 860 calle do Spade will be the only indication that this is the place you are looking for.

For more than twenty years, Giorgio Lanza and his family have been pouring wine while dispensing good cheer and wonderful snacks and sandwiches to their multitude of dedicated returnees, many of whom consider this to be their semi-private club. Over 220 wines are available by the glass, along with wild boar ham, salted cod, fish lasagna, and the Do Spade Sandwich, spicy ham covered with fresh herbs and piled onto crusty bread. For a slice of the real Venice without pretense, you can hardly get more authentic than this.

Da Marco
campiello del Sansoni, 900

AREA
San Polo
TELEPHONE
52.26.565
OPEN
Tues–Sun lunch and dinner
CLOSED
Mon; Jan 1–15; Aug
HOURS
Lunch noon–2:30 P.M., dinner 7:30–10 P.M.

Venetians know all about Da Marco's pizzas, but until now, most tourists did not. The list of pizzas is short but top drawer, especially the Gorgonzola with tomato, mozzarella, blue cheese, and onions, or the *alla Marco* with tomato, mozzarella, green peas, corn, and sausage. If pizza doesn't hit the spot, the only alternative is a calzone, a lavishly stuffed pizza bursting with two kinds of cheese, mushrooms, and ham.

The pizzas are served for lunch and dinner at long wooden tables that have paper covers over red linen cloths. The booths in the back room are made from old bed headboards collected by owner Claudio over the years. It is easy to see that he is a jazz-music enthusiast by the displays of original sheet music, photos of jazz greats, and baritone horns hanging all over the place. When you leave, be sure to notice his National Cash Register from Dayton, Ohio.

Do Mori
calle do Mori, 429 (off ruga Vecchia S. Giovanni)

For a glimpse of where the Rialto traders, delivery boys, and bank tellers go for wine and camaraderie, look no further than the Cantina do Mori.

Inside it is long, narrow, dark, and smoky. Hams hanging from low beams, a stand-up bar (there are no tables at all), great *cicchetti*, platters of local salami and prosciutto, enormous sandwiches, 350 wines to taste, and more decidedly male atmosphere than you will find almost anywhere else are part of this traditional old wine bar. In existence since 1462 it is now run by knowledgeable wine expert Roberto Biscontin. He will be happy to advise you on which wines you should drink with whatever you are eating. For instance, if it is salt cod, it should be a glass of Prosecco. With the winter sausage and beans, you will need a robust Cabernet.

Ignazio
calle Saoneri, 2749

Ignazio serves some of the best food you will have in Venice. Just ask anyone who has ever eaten there and they all agree—I know I do.

Everything is impressive, from the host's warm greeting to the last forkful of dessert. Ignazio has been a family-run restaurant for four decades and enjoys patronage from a devoted clientele that ranges from sophisticated, traditional businesspeople to casual couples busy falling in love all over again. Great pains are taken to lay a handsome table using delicate china,

RESERVATIONS
Advised for dinner on weekend
CREDIT CARDS
None
À LA CARTE
L 9,000, beverage not included
MENÙ TURISTICO
None
ENGLISH
Yes
COVER & SERVICE CHARGES
L 2,000, 12% service charge

AREA
San Polo
TELEPHONE
52.25.401
OPEN
Thurs–Wed
CLOSED
Wed afternoon; Sun; holidays; July 15–Aug 15
HOURS
8:30 A.M.–1:30 P.M. and 5–8:30 P.M.
RESERVATIONS
Not accepted
CREDIT CARDS
None
À LA CARTE
L 1,800 and up for sandwiches and snacks, beverage not included
MENÙ TURISTICO
None
ENGLISH
Some
COVER & SERVICE CHARGES
No cover or service charge

AREA
San Polo
TELEPHONE
52.34.852
OPEN
Sun–Fri lunch and dinner
CLOSED
Sat; second 2 weeks July; first 2 weeks March
HOURS
Lunch noon–3 P.M., dinner 7–10 P.M.

RESERVATIONS
Necessary for both lunch and
dinner
CREDIT CARDS
AMEX, DC, MC, V
À LA CARTE
L 40,000, beverage not
included
MENÙ TURISTICO
None
ENGLISH
Yes
COVER & SERVICE CHARGES
L 2,500 cover, 12% service
charge

gleaming glassware, and attractive silver. In the summer, there is an added bonus of a leafy green outdoor garden for al fresco dining. The English-speaking waiters always carry out their duties with professionalism and considerable style.

One taste of the food, prepared by three hard-working female chefs, and you will know you are in good hands. The meal begins with an assortment of *antipasti*, perhaps huge prawns bathed in a lemon and oil dressing or prosciutto with cool slices of melon. For the first course, I recommend their special *spaghetti alla trapanese*: egg pasta mixed with eggplant, peppers, tomatoes, and garlic, and tossed in a light cream sauce. Although fish is king here, with the fresh salmon and sole heading the list, meat eaters have not been forgotten with the Venetian-style sautéed liver and onions, and the grilled filet mignon. Desserts, so often the least distinguished part of an Italian meal, are excellent, especially the warm pear tart, their specialty, and the homemade *tiramisù*, that rich Venetian favorite made with Mascarpone, a sweet triple-cream cheese.

Prices at Ignazio tend to run a little high, so if cost is a factor, keep it for a special occasion.

Note: Ignazio belongs to the Ristoranti della Buona Accoglienza. For an explanation of this independent restaurateurs' organization devoted to good value and quality food, see Ai Gondolieri, page 114.

Trattoria Pizzeria San Tomà
campo San Tomà, 2864

AREA
San Polo
TELEPHONE
52.38.819
OPEN
Wed–Mon lunch and dinner
CLOSED
Tues; Nov 15–Dec 15;
Feb 1–15

Good pizza, delicious homemade pastas, a better-than-average *menù turistico*, friendly waiters offering good service, a beautiful lighted garden, and an outside dining terrace on the piazza that is perfect for people-watching all work together to create a memorable dining experience at Bernardo Di-Zio's Trattoria. If you arrive just before lunchtime, you might see the linguine, *tagliatelle*, and *pappardelle* out drying in the sun. Also on the menu are the usual Venetian standards of marinated sardines, fried fish, and liver with polenta. Because the servings are he-man in size, dessert is kept to a minimum, with the emphasis on *sorbet, tartufo,* and fresh fruit.

The only drawback is the cover and service charges, which can bump the price over the edge for most Cheap Eater budgets. However, with careful shopping, a reasonable repast is possible. The good news is that a full three-course meal is *not* necessary. You can just have pasta and salad and still be treated as though you were ordering the works.

HOURS
Lunch noon–3 P.M.,
dinner 7–10 P.M.
RESERVATIONS
Advised for Sat, Sun, holidays
CREDIT CARDS
AMEX, DC, MC, V
À LA CARTE
L 35,000, full meal, beverage
not included
MENÙ TURISTICO
L 20,000, 3 courses, beverage
not included
COVER & SERVICE CHARGES
L 2,000 cover, 12% service
charge

RESTAURANTS IN SANTA CROCE
   Ae Oche
   Brodo di Giuggiole
   La Zucca
   Trattoria alle Burchielle

Ae Oche
calle del Tintor, 1552 A–B

Ae Oche is young, fun, cheap, and good. This traditional gathering ground for the Italian yuppie fast-food generation is *never* empty. I have yet to find a way to beat the Sunday crowd of contented families who pile in for its fifty-three varieties of crisp pizzas. You can dine outside on a little deck, in a tented garden in the back, or at one of the inside booths.

The *Disco Volante* (flying saucer), two pizzas put together sandwich style, is not a stellar choice and neither is the house wine. You are better off with a beer. Fire-eaters will love pizza No. 15, the *mangiafuoco,* with spicy salami, hot chilies, paprika, and Tabasco. Those with tamer taste buds will opt for No. 10, the *fondelli,* with tomato, mozzarella, sausage, and ricotta cheese.

There is also a regular trattoria menu with *antipasti,* pastas, omelettes, meats, and salads. The long list of desserts will appeal to everyone who is not sticking to a rigid diet.

AREA
Santa Croce
TELEPHONE
52.41.161
OPEN
Tues–Sun lunch and dinner
CLOSED
Mon; Aug 8–31; 2 weeks at
Christmas and New Year's
HOURS
Lunch noon–3 P.M.,
dinner 7–10:30 P.M.
RESERVATIONS
Not accepted
CREDIT CARDS
MC, V
À LA CARTE
L 3,800–12,000 pizzas,
beverage not included;
L 23,000 regular menu,
beverage not included
MENÙ TURISTICO
None
ENGLISH
Yes
COVER & SERVICE CHARGES
L 1,000 cover, 12% service
charge

Brodo di Giuggiole
fondamenta Minotto, 158

AREA
Santa Croce
TELEPHONE
52.42.486
OPEN
Thurs–Tues lunch and dinner
CLOSED
Wed; NAC
HOURS
Lunch noon–2:30 P.M.,
dinner 7:30–10:30 P.M.
RESERVATIONS
Suggested for Sat and Sun
CREDIT CARDS
AMEX, DC, MC, V
À LA CARTE
L 35,000, beverage not
included
MENÙ TURISTICO
None
ENGLISH
Yes
COVER & SERVICE CHARGES
No cover or service charge

New and recommended, this Cheap Eat exclusive is owned by longtime restaurateur Irina Freguia. She has taken a tired old spot not far from piazzale Roma and turned it into an eye-catching winner that reminds me of a place you would expect to find in California. The stark white walls, yellow tablecloths, black bentwood chairs with cane seats, white china, fresh flowers, a nonsmoking section, and an outside dining patio in back create a casual and appealing atmosphere. The informally dressed waiters, wearing Levis and wild ties, have an upbeat attitude that goes a long way toward making everyone feel welcome.

The food is an imaginative mix of Venetian standbys, with the emphasis on vegetables and fondues. To begin, try the assorted vegetables dipped in egg batter and deep-fried, or the light vegetable soufflé. The unusual pastas have a limited appeal. Better to have the lentil soup or skip this course entirely and order a fondue for two—maybe the *bourguignonne* or the *vigneron*. Accomplished carnivores can dig into a T-bone steak, a mixed grill, or *Carpaccio*: thinly sliced raw beef served with a piquant sauce. For dessert, I loved the *brodo di Giuggiole,* floating island in a sea of soft custard, and the chocolate fondue with fresh and dried fruits for dipping. While prices for the fondues and main courses may appear high at first glance, remember that the meat dishes are garnished, and all the prices on the menu include the cover and service charges.

La Zucca
San Giacomo dell'Orio, 1762

AREA
Santa Croce
TELEPHONE
52.41.570
OPEN
Mon–Sat lunch and dinner

Collectors of unusual cuisine take note: this may be your only chance to sample pumpkin pasta, a tasty treat from which this appealing little trattoria takes its name. Unfortunately, you will have to time your visit in the fall or winter, because it is only a seasonal dish. The rest of the menu shows imagination and originality, and while not everything works all the time, most of it does. The menu changes often, and the four young and enthusiastic owners strive to please a savvy group of youthful habitués. Topping their best creations are the *gnocchi* stuffed with either feta cheese and served with a sweet-pepper sauce, or stuffed with dried ricotta and served in an eggplant and tomato sauce. The turkey burger leaves one wondering, but the fricasseed rabbit in a lemon sauce is outstanding and so are the creamy leek gratinée and the cauliflower vinaigrette. For dessert, the frozen yogurt with fresh raspberry sauce and the chocolate mousse are first class in their simplicity.

I think the best seating is toward the back at a window table on the rio delle Megio canal, rather than up front in the wine bar where the shoulder-to-shoulder crowd can get a little loud at times. When you go, be sure to take a good look at the modern paintings of pumpkins in every guise imaginable that line the oak paneled walls.

CLOSED
Sun; Aug 15-31; between Christmas and New Year's

HOURS
Lunch noon–3 P.M., dinner 7–11 P.M.

RESERVATIONS
Suggested for dinner

CREDIT CARDS
None

À LA CARTE
L 31,000, beverage not included

MENÙ TURISTICO
None

ENGLISH
Yes

COVER & SERVICE CHARGES
L 2,500 cover, no service charge

Trattoria alle Burchielle
Tre Ponti, fondamenta Burchielle, 393

Fifty years ago Pagin Bruno's uncle opened Trattoria alle Burchielle. Now under Bruno and his niece Serena's direction, it is still going strong as a local favorite best known for its fine fish. The restaurant sits alongside a pretty canal in a picturesque corner of Venice, not too far from piazzale Roma. On a summer evening, it is lovely to sit outside under the Venice moon and watch the boats drifting by while enjoying textbook examples of traditional Venetian preparations of fresh fish. Noteworthy among the first courses are the seafood lasagna and the spaghetti with whole clams. The most popular main-course offerings are the *sogliola ai ferri*—grilled sole—and the giant prawns bathed in a lemon, garlic, and olive oil marinade. Sweets adorn the pastry cart, but they are not made in house. A nice change of pace for dessert is a selection of Italian cheeses. The menu is translated into English, but if you can understand restaurant Italian at all, ask for the Italian version because it lists more.

AREA
Santa Croce

TELEPHONE
51.31.342

OPEN
Tues–Sun lunch and dinner

CLOSED
Mon; Jan

HOURS
Lunch noon–3 P.M., dinner 7–10 P.M.

RESERVATIONS
Advised

CREDIT CARDS
AMEX, MC, V

À LA CARTE
L 28,000, beverage not included

MENÙ TURISTICO
None

ENGLISH
Yes

COVER & SERVICE CHARGES
L 1,500 cover, 10% service charge

LA GIUDECCA

La Giudecca is where the wealthiest aristocrats of early Renaissance Venice built their homes. Today the island is a mixture of crumbling rundown buildings side by side with beautifully restored ones with lovely gardens. La Giudecca is hardly on the A list for the tourist, but it is interesting in its own quiet way. From the Zattere vaporetto stop in Venice, take No.5 or No.8 and get off at S. Eufemia or Giudecca.

RESTAURANTS ON LA GIUDECCA
Altanella

Altanella
rio de Ponte Lungo, 268

AREA	Giudecca Island
TELEPHONE	52.27.780
OPEN	Wed–Sun lunch and dinner
CLOSED	Mon; Tues; Jan to Carnival; Aug 10–20
HOURS	Lunch 12:30–2 P.M., dinner 7:30–9 P.M.
RESERVATIONS	Essential in summer
CREDIT CARDS	None
À LA CARTE	L 36,000, beverage not included
MENÙ TURISTICO	None
ENGLISH	Yes
COVER & SERVICE CHARGES	L 2,000 cover, 10% service charge

Altanella has what Italians call a *buona forchetta* ("a good fork") and a *buon bicchiere* ("a good glass"). Hidden on a narrow street on Giudecca Island, the Stradella family restaurant has been in business for four decades, preparing *only* fish. It looks undiscovered, but is firmly on the map. Even François Mitterand eats here whenever he is in Venice. However, fame has not gone to anyone's head—the food and prices are both still marvelous.

During warm weather, reserve a table on the irresistibly romantic terrace overlooking the island's central canal. Otherwise, you can sit at one of the tables inside, where you can look at photos of the restaurant in its early days and see the photo of the founder that hangs over the kitchen door. Whatever you order will be well prepared and properly served. Dishes I look forward to trying again are the risotto with fish, the pasta with cuttlefish or mussels and sweet peppers, the grilled sea bream, and the flavorful tuna. The desserts are made here, so be sure to plan on a piece of the lush chocolate cake or the lighter-than-usual *tiramisù*.

Because fish in Venice is *always* expensive, the prices here are above most Cheap Eaters' daily budgets, but for a moderate Big Splurge, Altanella is a lovely selection.

LIDO

Mention the Lido, across the lagoon from Venice, and everyone thinks of an exclusive and expensive resort. Today it still can be *very* expensive, even though it has lost a great deal of its former luster and chic appeal.

RESTAURANTS ON THE LIDO
Favorita
Pizzeria da Massimo
Ristorante Belvedere e Tavola Calda

Favorita
via Francesco Duodo, 33

The regulars at Favorita come for the good wine and the homespun food turned out by a hard-working squad of women chefs. Hidden in a pretty residential district about twenty minutes from the vaporetto stop from Venice, this appealing restaurant has been feeding Lido residents and visitors for three decades. Summer seating on the vine-covered terrace is always in great demand, but the seats are hard plastic without cushions, and thus not many deals are made or romances begun while eating here. The inside is more comfortable. The two large rooms have great atmosphere, with their heavy beams, nice collection of country furniture, liberal use of green plants and fresh floral arrangements, and soft pink table linens. The kitchen does not offer daily specials; instead it concentrates on doing a superb job with everything listed on the sensible menu. The emphasis is on fish. In fact, if you are not a fish eater, you have only two entrée choices: a steak or an omelette. The *gnocchi* with crab is perfect, and so is the spaghetti with fresh clams. Grilled eel, filet of sole, scampi, calamari, bass, and turbot make up the best fish main courses. The desserts do not inspire, but if something sweet is called for, *gelato* or *sorbetto* fills the bill.

AREA
Lido

TELEPHONE
52.61.626

OPEN
Tues–Sun lunch and dinner

CLOSED
Mon, Jan

HOURS
Lunch 12:30–2:30 P.M., dinner 7:30–10:30 P.M.

RESERVATIONS
Essential

CREDIT CARDS
AMEX, DC, MC, V

À LA CARTE
L 32,000, beverage not included

MENÙ TURISTICO
None

ENGLISH
Yes

COVER & SERVICE CHARGES
L 3,000 cover, 12% service charge

Pizzeria da Massimo
riviera S. Nicolo, 11A

AREA
Lido

TELEPHONE
52.60.859

OPEN
Wed–Mon lunch and dinner

CLOSED
Tues; annual closing varies

HOURS
Lunch 12:30–2 P.M.,
dinner 7–10 P.M.

RESERVATIONS
Not necessary

CREDIT CARDS
None

À LA CARTE
L 25,000, beverage not
included; L 15,000 pizza and
salad, beverage not included

MENÙ TURISTICO
L 20,000, 3 courses, beverage
not included

ENGLISH
Yes

COVER & SERVICE CHARGES
L 1,500 cover, no service charge

Pizzerias are a dime a dozen on the Lido, and almost all are touristy in the worst sense—you just cannot escape it. The pizzeria da Massimo is a more local spot than most. Just a few minutes from all the tourist hype on the main street, it offers decent pizza in a clean, informal setting. In summer it is especially nice to sit on the outside terrace and enjoy your food while soaking up the view across the canal, or gazing at all the people strolling by in various forms of dress, or undress, depending on the temperature. Twenty-five varieties of pizza are sold here, ranging from the ever-present tomato and mozzarella with a sprinkling of oregano, to the Inferno with garlic, hot salami, and peppers, and the Della Casa starring tomato, cheese, mushrooms, ham, and eggplant. The desserts are not worth worrying about, but after a big pizza and a salad, you won't have much room left over anyway. There is also a set-price menu and an à la carte menu, but choices are boring on both—best to think *only* pizza here.

Ristorante Belvedere e Tavola Calda
piazzale la Santa Maria Elisabetta, 4

AREA
Lido

TELEPHONE
52.60.115, 52.60.164

OPEN
Tues–Sun lunch and dinner

CLOSED
Mon; Nov to April

HOURS
Lunch noon–2:30 P.M.,
dinner 7–9 P.M.

RESERVATIONS
Advised for *ristorante*, not
accepted at *tavola calda*

CREDIT CARDS
AMEX, DC, MC, V

À LA CARTE
L 45,000 *ristorante*, beverage
not included; L 15,000 *tavola
calda*, beverage included

If you are visiting the Lido for the day, chances are you will want to have a meal. Most of the food is overpriced tourist pizza or deadly dull and ludicrously expensive hotel dining; there does not seem to be much of a middle ground. Enter the Ristorante Belvedere and its Tavola Calda snack bar next door. Everyone agrees that some of the best food to be had in this tourist mecca is at the Belvedere, right across the street from the vaporetto stop from Venice. At the restaurant, Cheap Eaters will order the *menù turistico*, a L 25,000 value that includes three courses, dessert, and wine or mineral water. The food, which features marvelous fresh fish, is served on a pretty street-side terrace or in the formal hotel dining room with big picture windows. Card-carrying Cheap Eaters will head straight for the Tavola Calda that adjoins the more expensive restaurant. The same kitchen is used at both places, but the prices here are much lower. Every day there are pastas, roast chicken, fish, and an excellent selection of vegetables and salads, plus made-to-order sandwiches. Tavola Calda is just the answer for the visitor with lots on the agenda and no time or desire for a fancy meal.

MENÙ TURISTICO
Ristorante: L 25,000, all courses, wine or mineral water; *tavola calda*: none
ENGLISH
Yes
COVER & SERVICE CHARGES
L 3,500 cover at *ristorante*, no service charge; no cover or service charge at *tavola calda*

MURANO

Murano has been the home of Venetian glass-making since the thirteenth century. Visitors are welcome to watch glass blowers at work in one of the many factories on the island. However, *please* watch for the high-pressure tactics used to lure customers from Venice to specific factories. Avoid all "special" boats to Murano, and take No.5 from fondamenta Nuove.

RESTAURANTS ON MURANO
Ai Vetrai
Antica Trattoria Muranese

Ai Vetrai
fondamenta Manin, 29

Forty-seven years ago Sergio Scarpa opened Ai Vetrai. Then it was a small restaurant with only a few tables, serving fresh fish to locals and visitors on the island of Murano. The years have changed things—dramatically. Now there are seats for two hundred people in several rooms and on an outside terrace facing a canal. The menu is printed in four languages, and most of the waiters are at least bilingual. While he has expanded his operation, Sergio has not changed his goal: to provide friendly service and the best meat and fish he can find at fair and reasonable prices. The *menù turistico* at L 20,000 for all courses, including the wine, is one of the best Cheap Eats on Murano. Daily specials, in addition to fresh fish, include ravioli with spinach and ricotta cheese, spaghetti with whole clams, and *risotto de pesche* (risotto with fish). Some of

AREA
Murano
TELEPHONE
73.92.93
OPEN
Fri–Wed lunch and dinner
CLOSED
Evenings in winter; Thurs; Jan
HOURS
Winter 11:30 A.M.–5 P.M., summer 11:30 A.M.–11 P.M.
RESERVATIONS
Not necessary
CREDIT CARDS
AMEX, DC, MC, V
À LA CARTE
L 30,000, beverage not included
MENÙ TURISTICO
L 20,000, 3 courses, beverage included

the better meat entrées are the stewed veal or beef, the veal Marsala, and the *entrecôte* with mushrooms. In the summer, the restaurant offers continuous food service from 11:30 A.M. until 11:00 P.M., a real boon to the many visitors who have different meal schedules.

Antica Trattoria Muranese
fondamenta Cavour, 20

Situated on the canal about halfway down from the Venice vaporetto stop is the Antica Trattoria Muranese, a reliable bet for an unassuming seafood lunch in Murano. Not much on this island, so famous for its glass, caters to the locals, but at least the food and service here are good and honest. The pretty summer garden in back with tables and umbrellas adds to warm-weather dining pleasure. Recommended picks for Cheap Eaters are the set-price menu (not always displayed, so ask for it if you don't see it), and an à la carte pasta and a mixed salad. Haute cuisine is not part of the kitchen creed, so for maximum results, think simple. Rely on the grilled fish rather than the heavily breaded and fried versions, and order a green salad or the veggie of the day rather than one that has been frozen. All the fish is purchased at the Rialto fish market, and whatever is freshest that day will be the special. The uninteresting bakery desserts make it easy to bypass this course. Instead, treat yourself to a *gelato* while strolling around the island and shopping for glass mementos to take home.

QUICK REFERENCE GUIDE

BIG SPLURGE

GLOSSARY OF WORDS, PHRASES, AND MENU TERMS

BIG SPLURGE

These are more-expensive restaurants, included for those who have flexible budgets and want something special. These restaurants range in price from 35,000 *lire* and up per person, without wine, for an à la carte meal of at least three courses.

FLORENCE

Cafaggi	33
Cantinetta Antinori	25
Croce al Trebbio	25
Taverna del Bronzino	36
Trattoria da Tito	23

ROME

Albino il Sardo	83
Antico Bottaro	69
Del Giglio	77
Girarrosto Toscano	89
Mario	96
Orso '80	67
Osteria ar Galletto	65
Re degli Amici	97

VENICE

Ai Gondolieri	114
Al Covo	110
Al Gobbo di Rialto	126
All'Antico Pizzo	128
Bella Venezia	106
Brodo di Giuggiole	134
Da Nico	121
Fiore	122
Ignazio	131
Il Melograno	108
Sempione	125
Trattoria Pizzeria San Tomà	132

GIUDECCA

Altanella	136

LIDO

Ristorante Belvedere e Tavola Calda	138

GLOSSARY OF WORDS, PHRASES, AND MENU TERMS

Here are some words and phrases to help you further enjoy *Cheap Eats in Italy.*

WORDS AND PHRASES

Hello (telephone)	*pronto*
Hello/goodbye (familiar)	*ciao*
Good morning	*buon giorno*
Good afternoon	*buon pomeriggio*
Good evening	*buona sera*
Good night	*buona notte*
Goodbye	*arrivederci*
Please	*per favore*
Thank you	*grazie*
You are welcome	*prego*
Yes/no	*si/no*
Excuse me	*mi scusi*
Do you speak English?	*parla inglese?*
I don't speak Italian	*non parlo italiano*
I understand	*capisco*
I don't understand	*non capisco*
Today, tonight, tomorrow	*oggi, stasera, domani*
Where are the restrooms?	*dov'è la toilette [per signore (women), per signori (men)]*
How much is it?	*quanto costa?*
a little/ a lot	*poco/tanto*
more/less	*più/meno*
enough/too much	*abbastanza/troppo*
open/closed	*aperto/chiuso*
Waiter/waitress	*cameriere/cameriera*
Breakfast	*colazione*
Lunch	*pranzo*
Dinner	*cena*
The menu, please	*la lista, per favore*
The wine list, please	*la lista dei vini, per favore*
The bill, please	*il conto, per favore*
Is the service included?	*il servizio è incluso?*
Service is included	*il servizio è compreso/incluso*
Service is not included	*il servizio non è compreso/incluso*
Please telephone for a taxi	*per favore, telefoni per un tassi*
No smoking	*vietato fumare*
First courses	*primi piatti*
Second courses	*secondi piatti*

Fixed-price menu	*menù turistico; prezzo fisso*
Dish of the day	*piatto del giorno*
Specialty of the house	*specialità della casa*
In season	*di stagione*
knife	*cotello*
fork	*forchetta*
spoon	*cucchiaio*
cup	*tazza*
plate	*piatto*
glass	*bicchiere*
bottle	*bottiglia*
ashtray	*portacenere*
chair	*sedia*
table	*tavola*
napkin	*il tovagliolo*
I would like	*vorrei*
a glass of	*un bicchiere di*
a bottle of	*una bottiglia di*
a 1/2 bottle of	*una mezza bottiglia di*
a carafe of	*una caraffa di*
a liter of	*uno litro di*
I am hungry	*ho fame*
I am diabetic	*ho il diabete*
I am on a diet	*sono a dieta*
I am vegetarian	*sono vegetariano (a)*
I cannot eat	*non posso mangiare*
It is hot/cold	*è caldo/freddo*
Please give me	*per favore, mi dia*
boiled	*bollito/lesso*
cooked	*cotto*
cooked in wine	*brasato*
firm, not overcooked, as in pasta	*al dente*
fried	*fritto*
frozen	*surgelato*
grilled	*alla griglia/ferri*
on the spit	*allo spiedo*
rare	*al sangue/poco cotto*
raw	*crudo*
roast	*arrosto*
smoked	*affumicato*
steamed/stewed	*umido*
stuffed	*ripieno*
well-done	*ben cotto*

TYPES OF PASTA

bigoli	round, solid pasta (Venice)
bucatini	hollow spaghetti
cannelloni	stuffed pasta tubes
capelli d'angelo	angel hair pasta
conchiglie	pasta shells
crespelle	crêpes
farfalle	butterfly-shaped pasta
fettuccine	long, thin pasta noodles
fusilli	spiral-shaped pasta
lasagne	large, flat noodles layered with ingredients and baked
maccheroni	macaroni
orecchiette	ear-shaped pasta
paglia e fieno	green and yellow tagliatelle
pappardelle	wide noodles
pasta verde	spinach noodles
pasticcio	baked pasta pie with cheese, vegetables, and meat
penne	narrow, diagonally cut macaroni
ravioli	filled pasta squares
rigatoni	large macaroni
rotelle	spiral-shaped pasta
tagliatelle	thin, flat egg pasta ribbons
taglierini	thin pasta ribbons
tagliolini	thin, flat noodles
tonarrelli	square-shaped spaghetti
tortelli	ravioli with a filling of potato or spinach and ricotta cheese
tortellini	small meat-filled pasta dumplings
tortellone	large tortellini
vermicelli	thin spaghetti
zite, ziti	short, wide, tube-shaped pasta

MENU TERMS

A

abbacchio	milk-fed lamb
acciughe	anchovies
aceto	vinegar
acqua cotta	thick vegetable soup poured over bread
acqua minerale (gassata, naturale)	mineral water (sparkling, still)
affettato	sliced
affumicato	smoked
aglio	garlic
agnello	lamb
agrume	citrus fruit
albicocca	apricot
al carbone	charcoal grilled
alici	anchovies
alimentari	grocery store
alla, all'	in the style of, with
all'amatriciana	with a sauce of bacon, tomatoes, onion, and hot pepper
all'arrabbiata	with a spicy, hot tomato sauce
alla brace	charcoal grilled
alla bucaniera	with a pasta sauce with seafood, tomato, garlic, parsley, and oil
alla cacciatora	with a sauce of tomato, onion, peppers, mushrooms, garlic, herbs, and wine
ananas	pineapple
anatra	duck
aneto	dill
anguilla	eel
antipasto	appetizer
antipasti misto	assorted appetizers
a piacere	as you like it
aperitivo	aperitif
aragosta	lobster, crayfish
arancia	orange
aringa	herring
arrosto	roast
asciutto	dry
asparagi	asparagus
assaggio	a taste
assagi	a series of small portions

B

baccalà	dried salt cod
bacelli	fava beans (Tuscan)
barbabietola	beet
Bel Paese	soft, mild cheese
bietole	Swiss chard
birra	beer
biscotti	cookies
bistecca	beef steak
bistecca alla fiorentina	T-bone steak, grilled over coals, and served very rare
bollito misto	mixed boiled meats
braciola	steak, chop, slice of meat
branzino	seabass
bresaola	air-cured beef, thinly sliced
briosca	croissant (also called cornetto)
brodetto	fish soup
brodo	broth
bruschetta	toasted garlic bread topped with tomatoes
bue	beef, ox
burro	butter

C

cacciagione	game
calamaro (calamaretto)	squid (baby squid)
caldo	hot/warm
calzone	stuffed pizza
camomilla	camomile tea
cannellini	white beans
caponata	eggplant salad
cappa santa	scallop
capperi	capers
capra (capretto)	goat (baby)
capriolo	venison
carbonade	beef stewed with red wine
carbonara	pasta sauce with bacon, eggs, Parmesan cheese
carciofo (alla giudia)	artichoke (deep-fried)
carne	meat
Carpaccio	thinly sliced raw beef
casalinga	home style
cavolfiore	cauliflower
cavolo (nero)	cabbage (red)
ceci	chick-peas
cervella	brains
cicchetti	snacks served with glass of wine (Venice)

ciliegia	cherry
cinghiale	wild boar
cioccolato	chocolate
cioccolato caldo	hot chocolate
cipolla	onion
cocomero	watermelon
coda di bue alla vaccinara	oxtail stew
coda di roposso	monkfish
congelato	frozen
coniglio	rabbit
contorni	side dishes (vegetables, salads, potatoes)
coperto	cover charge added per person to bill
cornetti	croissants, also called *briosche*
cotoletta	chop or cutlet
cozze	mussels
crema	custard
crespelle	crêpes
crostata	open-faced fruit tart
crostini	toasted bread spread with pâté, etc.
crudo	raw (as in *prosciutto crudo*: raw ham)
cucina	kitchen, cooking
cuore	heart

D

da portare via	to take out
degustazione	tasting
di stagione	of the season
dolce	dessert

E

enoteca	wine shop/bar
erbe	herbs

F

fagiano	pheasant
fagioli	beans
fagiolini	string beans
fave	fava beans
fegatelli	pork livers
fegatini	chicken livers
fegato	calves' liver
fettunta	garlic bread made with fresh olive oil (Florence)
fichi	figs
filetto	filet
finocchio	fennel

fior di zucca, fiori di zucchino	stuffed and fried zucchini flowers
focaccia	flat bread
Fontina	delicate, buttery cheese
forchetta	fork
formaggio	cheese
fragole	strawberries
fragoline	tiny wild strawberries
freddo	cold
fritelle	fritters
frittata	unfolded omelette
fritto	fried
fritto misto	assorted deep-fried foods (fish, vegetables)
frutta	fruit
frutti di mare	shellfish
funghi	mushrooms
funghi porcini	wild boletus mushrooms

G

gamberetti	shrimp
gastronomia	grocery store
gelato	ice cream
gianduia	chocolate and hazelnut (usually in ice cream)
gnocchi, gnocchetti	small potato dumplings served as pasta course
Gorgonzola	blue-veined cheese
granchio	crab
grappa	alcoholic spirit distilled from grape mash
grissini	bread sticks

H

Hag	brand name of the most popular decaf coffee, used to mean decaffeinated in general

I

imbottito	stuffed
insalata	salad
insalata caprese	salad made with tomatoes, mozzarella, basil, vinegar, lemon, and olive oil
integrale	whole wheat
involtini	stuffed meat or fish rolls

L

lampone	raspberries

latte	milk
latteria	store selling dairy products
lenticchie	lentils
lepre	wild hare
lesso	boiled
limone	lemon
lombatine	veal chop
lumache	snails

M

macedonia	fresh fruit chopped and served with dessert
maiale	pork
mandorla	almond
manzo	beef
ministra	soup

N

nazionale	domestic, meaning made in Italy
noce	walnut
nocciola	hazelnut

O

oca	goose
olio di oliva	olive oil

P

pane	bread
panna	cream
panino	sandwich
patata	potato
pollo	chicken
prosciutto	air-dried, salt-cured ham
prosciutto cotto	cooked, air-dried, salt-cured ham
prosciutto crudo	raw, dried, salt, air-cured ham
provolone	a smooth cow's-milk cheese
prunga	plum
prunga secca	prune
putanesca	"prostitute's style" sauce with tomatoes, capers, red peppers, anchovies, and garlic
puntarelle	wild chicory greens
purè di patate	mashed potatoes

R

radicchio	red chicory
ragù	meat sauce (for pasta)
rape	turnip greens

ravanello	radish
ribollita	bean, bread, cabbage, and vegetable soup (Florence)
ricotta	soft, mild sheep's cheese
ripieno	stuffed
risi e bisi	thick pea and rice soup
riso	rice
risotto	sautéed rice cooked slowly in broth with vegetables or fish added

S

semifreddo	ice cream cake
sorbetto	sherbert

T

tè, thè	tea
tiramisù	rich, creamy dessert made with Mascarpone cheese, liqueur, espresso, chocolate, and ladyfingers (literally means "pick-me-up")
tisana	herbal tea
tonno	tuna
torta	cake
tostato	toasted
tramezzino	sandwich (also called *panino*)
trancia	slice
trippa	tripe
trota	trout

U

un'etto	100 grams, about 4 ounces
uova	egg
uva	grape

V

verdure	vegetables
verza	cabbage; also *cavolo*
vino (rosso, rosato, bianco)	wine (red, rosé, white)
vin santo	sweet dessert wine

READERS' COMMENTS

In *Cheap Eats in Italy*, I recommend places as they were when this book went to press and as I hope they will stay, but there are no guarantees. While every effort has been made to ensure the accuracy of the information presented, the reader must understand that prices, menu selections, opening and closing times, vacation schedules, and ownership all can change overnight. Therefore, the author and publisher cannot accept responsibility for changes that do occur.

Cheap Eats in Italy is updated and revised on a regular basis. If you find a change before I do, or make a discovery that you want to pass along, please send me a note stating the name and address of the restaurant, the date of your visit, and a description of your findings. Your comments are extremely important to me, and I follow through on every letter sent. Thank you.

Please send your letters to Sandra A. Gustafson (*Cheap Eats in Italy*), c/o Chronicle Books, 275 Fifth Street, San Francisco, CA 94103.

INDEX

A

Abruzzese   75
Acquacotta   24–25
Ae Oche   133
Ai Cugnai   113–14
Ai Gondolieri   114–15
Ai Promessi Sposi   105
Ai Vetrai   139–40
Albino il Sardo   83
Al Covo   110–11
Alemagna   72
Al Fagianetto   76
Al Fontanone   84
Al Gobbo di Rialto   126–27
Aliani Gastronomia   127
Alimentari   30
Alla Maddalena   105–6
Alla Madonna   127–28
All'Antico Pizzo   128–29
Almanacco (Centro Vegetariano Fiorentino)   32–33
Al Milion   129
Al Pompiere   62–63
Altanella   136
Antica Locanda Montin   115
Antica Trattoria da Nino   106
Antica Trattoria e Fiaschetteria   40
Antica Trattoria Muranese   140
Antichi Cancelli   33
Antico Bottaro   69–70
Antico Capon   116
Arancio d'Oro   93
Armando   30–31

B

Baccus   31–32
Baffetto   66
Bar Ricchi   40–41
Bar/Trattoria Santa Croce   46–47
Bella Roma   87–88

Bella Venezia   106–7
Belle Donne   25–26
Beltramme Fiaschetteria   93–94
Birreria Peroni   73
Bora Bora   121
Bottigliera Reali   76
breakfast   11
Brodo di Giuggiole   134
Buca dell'Orafo   44–45
Bucatino   74

C
Ca' d'Oro   107–8
Cafaggi   33–34
Caffè Caruso   54–55
Caffè dei Frari   129–30
Cantina do Spade   130
Cantinetta Antinori   26
CarLie's   47
Centro Macrobioto Italiano   94
Cip Ciap   111
coffee   12–13
cover charge   16–17
Crepizza   116–17
Croce al Trebbio   26–27

D
Da Benvenuto   48
Da Bepi   108
Da Franco ar Vicoletto   76
Da Giorgio   51
Da Giovanni Osteria e Cucina   84–85
Da Marco   130–31
Da Nico   121–22
Da Pennello   27
Del Giglio   77–78
Der Pallaro   64
dinner   11–12
Do Mori   131

E
Enoteca Cavour 313   60

F
Favorita   137
Fiaschetteria al Panino   48–49
Fiaschetteria Marini   78
Fiore   122–23
Friggitoria da Bruno   117

G

Gastronomia Vera	41
Gelati Nico	117–18
Gemma e Maurizio	78–79
Gino e Pietro	67
Gioia Mia	99
Giolitti	63
Giovanni Fassi, Palazzo del Freddo	79
Girarrosto Toscano	89
Gran Caffè la Strega	80

H

holidays	15
Hostaria da Paolo e Liliana	80–81
Hostaria dei Bastioni	90
Hostaria Giulio	64–65

I

I' Cchè C'é C'é	55
Ignazio	131–32
Il Barroccio	49–50
Il Cardellino	34–35
Il Contadino	51–52
Il Doge Gelaterie	118
Il Fornaio	45
Il Granduca	28
Il Melograno	108–9
Il Re del Tramezzino	81
Il Secchio	81–82
Il Triangolo delle Bermude	52
Insalata Ricca	65
Insalata Ricca 2	67
I Numeri	95
I Raddi	42

L

La Bottega del Vino	63
La Buca di Ripetta	70
La Falterona	35
La Gensola	85
La Lampara	52–53
La Macelleria	35–36
L'Archetto	73–74
La Zucca	134–35
Le Mossacce	28
Leon Bianco	123
Le Sorelle	24
L'Incontro	118–19
lunch	11

M

Marcello Osteria	99–100
Margutta Vegetariano	95–96
Mario	96
Mario's	85
menus	13–14
menu terms	147–52
Montecatini	55–56

O

Orso '80	67–68
Ostariada Nerone	60–61
Osteria ai Assassini	123–24
Osteria Ar Galletto	65–66
Osteria da Luciano	82
Osteria del Cinghiale Bianco	45–46
Osteria St. Ana	70–71

P

Palladini	68
Palle d'Oro	29
Paneformaggio	71
Paolin	124
pasta	146
Pasticceria d'Angelo	96–97
Pasticceria Marino	42–43
paying	16
Piccolo Arancio	88
Pizzeria da Massimo	138
Pizzeria Ivo	86
Pizzeria la Capricciosa	97
Pizzeria la Montecarlo	69
Pizzeria l'Economica	82–83
Pizzeria Panattoni	87
Premiata Latteria Zorzi	124–25
prices	16

R

Re degli Amici	97–98
reservations	15
Ristorante al Ponte	109–10
Ristorante Belvedere e Tavola Calda	138–39
Ristorante de' Medici	53
Rosticceria S. Bartolomeo	125

S

Santoro	71–72
Sempione	125–26
service charge	17
Settimio all'Arancio	98
smoking	16

T

Taverna dei Quaranta	61
Taverna del Bronzino	36–37
Taverna San Trovaso	119–20
Tavola d'Oro	90–91
Tonolo	120
Trattoria alle Burchielle	135
Trattoria Casalinga	43
Trattoria da Tito	23
Trattoria del Carmine	43–44
Trattoria Dino	91
Trattoria Enzo e Piero	37
Trattoria Gozzi	37–38
Trattoria Guelfa	53–54
Trattoria l'Albanese	61–62
Trattoria Mario	38–39
Trattoria Memmo	91–92
Trattoria Pizzeria San Tomà	132–33
Trattoria Rivetta	112
Trattoria Rondinella	92
Trattoria Tofanelli	112–13
Trattoria Zà Zà	39

V

Vini del Chianti	29
Vivoli	50

Other titles in the *Cheap Eats* and *Cheap Sleeps* travel series by Sandra A. Gustafson:

Cheap Eats in Paris
Cheap Sleeps in Paris
Cheap Eats in London
Cheap Sleeps in London

These and additional Chronicle Books titles are available at your local bookstore. For a color catalog of all our books, call or write:

Chronicle Books
275 Fifth Street
San Francisco, California 94103
1-800-722-6657